Let the Mountains Talk,
Let the Rivers Run

*A call to those who
would save the Earth*

David R. Brower

with Steve Chapple

New Society Publishers

To those already committed to healing the Earth
and to those about to be.

Cataloguing in Publication Data:
A catalog record for this publication is available from the National Library of Canada.

Copyright © 2000 by David Brower and Steve Chapple.
All rights reserved.
Second printing, 2001.
Original edition published in 1995 by HarperCollins Publishers, New York.

Book design by George Brown.

Cover design by Miriam MacPhail. Cover photograph by John Dyer of David Brower on the mast of
Shiprock, New Mexico, leading the first ascent, 1939.
Authors photograph by Kitti Homme.

This book is printed entirely on 60lb. totally chlorine-free, tree-free kenaf paper,
thanks to the generosity of Earth Island Institute and Vision Paper. For more
information, contact Earth Island Institute, 300 Broadway, Suite 28, San Francisco,
CA 94133; or Vision Paper, P.O. Box 20399, Albuquerque, New Mexico, 87154; or
www.visionpaper.com.
Printed in Canada using soy-based inks by Friesens.

New Society Publishers acknowledges the support of the Government of Canada through the Book
Publishing Industry Development Program (BPIDP) for our publishing activities, and the assistance
of the Province of British Columbia through the British Columbia Arts Council.

BRITISH
COLUMBIA
ARTS COUNCIL
Supported by the Province of British Columbia

Paperback ISBN: 0-86571-411-8

Inquiries regarding requests to reprint all or part of *Let The Mountains Talk, Let the Rivers Run* should be
addressed to New Society Publishers at the address below.
To order directly from the publishers, please add $4.50 shipping to the price of the first copy, and $1.00
shipping for each additional copy (plus GST in Canada). Send check or money order to:
New Society Publishers
P.O. Box 189, Gabriola Island, BC V0R 1X0, Canada

New Society Publishers aims to publish books for fundamental social change through nonviolent
action. We focus especially on sustainable living, progressive leadership, and educational and parent-
ing resources. Our full list of books can be browsed on the worldwide web at: www.newsociety.com

NEW SOCIETY PUBLISHERS
www.newsociety.com

Climb the mountains and get their good tidings.

—JOHN MUIR

Contents

Acknowledgments

WE WOULD LIKE TO THANK a number of people for taking time to share their thoughts in the middle of busy days and nights: Sam LaBudde, Jimmy Langman, John Knox, Justin Lowe, and Gar Smith of the Earth Island Institute; John Berger, Paul Hawken, Garrett DeBell, Amory Lovins, Kenneth Brower, Peter Warshall, Thomas Rymsza, Huey Johnson; Bob Ekey, communications director of the Greater Yellowstone Coalition, and Peter Aengst; Randy Hayes, director of the Rainforest Action Network: Michael Oppenheimer, senior scientist for the Environmental Defense Fund; Thomas J. Cassidy, general counsel, American Rivers; Mark Dowie, Richard Parker, and Will Nixon.

We are grateful to Quincey Tompkins Imhoff, executive director of the Foundation for Deep Ecology; Alfred Heller; and Thomas Wynett, for their generous financial support.

Chapple, especially, is thankful for the deadline indulgences of Karin Evans and Terry McDonell; the hospitality of Bea Vogel, Gil Bagot, Jr., Patti Bartlett, David and Isis Schwartz, David Helvarg and Nancy Ledansky; the good love of Kent McCarthy for Anchor Bay; and the usual extreme kindness shown by Maria Ines Pentagna Salgado, Cody, and Jack to his line of work.

Finally this book would not have made Earth Day on time without the encouragement of Chris Plant of New Society Publishers and Mikhail Davis, director of the Brower Fund, and the instincts of our agents, Ellen Levine and Anne Dubuisson.

Foreword
Amory B. Lovins

SOME WISE BIOLOGIST, perhaps E.O. Wilson, remarked that bees, ants, and termites, though not very smart individually, display much intelligence collectively—while people are just the opposite. Yet now and then, the search for intelligent life on Earth turns up a promising specimen—a much higher primate who, by combined force of logic and love, humor and passion, awakens the rest of us to our personal and especially our collective potential for enriching our habitat and each other.

Such a rare creature is David Brower, the greatest living environmentalist, among the greatest of all time—our generation's Thoreau or Emerson or Muir. His unique achievements are mainly described in terms of wilderness saved, lively organizations created in 50-odd countries, laws passed, attitudes changed, people inspired, publications issued, careers nurtured. Author Jerry Mander calls him "the most visionary, effective, and inspiring environmentalist of our age.... [I]t was his brand of no-compromise activism and thinking that has essentially vaulted the ecology movement into becoming a major international force." All correct, all incomplete. But those of us fortunate to have learned for decades from this master of natural philosophy and effective action, seasoned by his half-century at the forefront of the global environmental movement, are also especially happy to see the ripe and subtle intangible wisdom of his 88 years distilled into this book.

Before he led the building of the modern American, and indeed the global, environmental movement—the most obvious expression of his life's work—Dave's range of gifts emerged from equally diverse and complex challenges. As the eyes for his blind mother, he became a naturalist and aesthetician devoted to "mystery, the unending search for truth, the truth of beauty." As a leading mountaineer and co-inventor of ski mountaineering, he honed native boldness seasoned by judgment. As a soldier in World War II, rising in combat from private to major in the Tenth Mountain Division, he mastered leadership and organization. As an editor, he evolved clarity and grace. All these experiences, and more, fitted him to keep the gift moving, giving strategy and stamina to the thousands he continues to guide, instruct, and inspire.

We first met in London in 1969, when Philip Howell Evans—the great unsung Welsh landscape photographer—and I were advised by National Geographic to send our atmospheric mountain photographs to Dave because "he likes this sort of thing." Long in awe of his stunningly beautiful Exhibit Format books, which shaped our generation's appreciation of wild places, we hesitantly did so, hoping for the favor of a little advice. He liked our work, asking for more and for some writing. What a shock it was when at our next meeting, he gave us a half-hour to decide whether, over the next two months, we wanted to create one of his "big books." We'd never written, or photographed for, a book. He said it was time we started. He wanted me to do not only the writing but also the layout. I said I'd never done that. He said it was time I learned. He was right. The resulting book *Eryri, the Mountains of Longing* helped save a British National Park from despoliation by the world's largest mining company. The company never took our efforts to improve its financial performance in quite the gracious spirit in which they were meant, but did back off. Three decades later, having achieved mutual respect, we're exploring how to work together to make the firm a natural capitalist (www.naturalcapitalism.org).

Working with Dave on the book was a world-class graduate seminar in just about everything. Academic research was less interesting and far less important. Anyhow, Oxford wouldn't let me do a doctorate in energy policy—which, two years before the 1973 oil embargo, wasn't considered an academic subject; they had no chair in it. (They do now.) In 1971, moved by Dave's vision, I resigned from academia to work for him full-time—ultimately for a decade in London and another three years in the U.S., earning about enough to pay the phone bill, but offering complete freedom to choose tasks, priorities, and methods. All that mattered was quality, integrity, and results.

It was an adventure. We'd meet all over the world—in all-night strategy sessions, in airports, before Congressional committees, wherever. When Dave was coming to town, the proper equipment for going to see him included a toothbrush and passport, because there was no telling what airplane I'd be whisked aboard to go address the critical issue of the day. In those days, Friends of the Earth was largely a collection of talented people Dave had recruited, supported (too often from his own meager pocket), and given the freedom to do what they did best. The style was so far from bureaucratic as to verge on anarchic; the results were exceptional; the feeling was exhilarating; all became addictive.

My parents, I later discovered, were worried about my giving up an academic career; but they kindly kept it to themselves. It didn't matter. I'd entered a far more demanding and rewarding course of study and action, requiring one to pick up a couple of new disciplines a year. The final exam was effectiveness. I learned to do now what is necessary and important, how to influence others with diverse views and values, how things work, and what matters. Over the past half-century, hundreds if not thousands of young people have followed similar paths, joining this mentor who is at once charismatic and reflective, funny and profound. His commitment and personal interest have moved us all to give up safe, conventional, well-paying but unrewarding career tracks and to join his movement to save the world. That process continues unabated to this day as Dave continues to attract and enlist the talented youngsters who will strive to fill his giant shoes.

On rare occasions, we'd disagree about tactics, but I gradually learned that Dave was right; he was simply thinking ten years further ahead. He retains that uncanny prescience to this day. Still the most brilliantly visionary person I know, perpetually a decade or more ahead, he's asking and starting to answer the key questions that haven't yet occurred to the rest of us.

Dry humor falls like gentle rain through his speaking and writing. It's self-deprecatory, often with a sting in the tail, but never unkind. He's learned, as the environmental movement needs to learn, not to take itself too seriously. The underlying passion is still there too, but now more tolerantly accepting of mistakes (which are, as Edwin Land reminded us, "events not yet fully turned to one's advantage"). A few facts change, of course—the Hypercar™ described in this book is already starting to move into the marketplace (www.hypercarcenter.org)—but the underlying principles are perennial. Dave's insight into the majesties of life and the follies of politics is like a fine vintage, mellowing with age. The innate curiosity, optimism, risk-friendliness, and *joie de vivre* remain extraordinary. And the fine hand of Dave's wife Anne, also a brilliant editor, shines through the insights and the language.

In short, readers are in for a treat—for the privilege of learning why and how to commit themselves irrevocably to the brave and necessary agenda of global restoration. As the twenty-first century begins, it's too early to tell whether the recent upstart experiment of combining opposable thumbs with a large forebrain will turn out to be a good idea, but this book offers hope that it may. By leading what is now the global movement to sustain life, David Brower has already changed a myriad lives. This book could change yours, and hence those of all beings on Earth.

Old Snowmass, Colorado

February 5, 2000

CPR *for the* Earth:
An Invitation

I WAS STANDING beside Lester Brown, president of
the World Watch Institute, watching him sign copies of his
latest book at a store in Washington, D.C. Lester is a hero of mine.
In his early days as an agronomist in India, he once saved 10 million people from starving to death. He foresaw a crop failure and
was able to get the United States to ship one-fifth of its wheat
crop to avert the famine. That's something. On this day, he suddenly turned and asked me if I knew who had come up with the
quotation his publisher had put on the book's jacket: "We do not
inherit the Earth from our fathers, we are borrowing it from our
children."

"I have no idea," I replied.

"Those words," said Lester, "are carved in stone at the
National Aquarium, and your name is underneath them."

I was a bit pleased and thoroughly puzzled.

At home in California, I searched my unorganized files to find out when I could have said those words. I stumbled upon the answer in the pages of an interview that had taken place in a North Carolina bar so noisy, I could only marvel that I was heard at all. Possibly, I didn't remember saying it because by then they had me on my third martini.

I decided the words were too conservative for me. We're not borrowing from our children, we're *stealing* from them—and it's not even considered to be a crime.

Let that be my epitaph, when I need it.

In the years since the Industrial Revolution, we humans have been partying pretty hard. We've ransacked most of the Earth for resources. A small part of the world's population wound up with some nice goodies, but now we're eating the seed corn. We are living off the natural capital of the planet, the principal, and not the interest. The soil, the seas, the forests, the rivers, and the protective atmospheric cover—all are being depleted. It was a grand binge, but the hangover is now upon us, and it will soon be throbbing.

To our unborn children, it will seem that we did, indeed, burn books to get light, burn furniture to run air-conditioning, and burn arbors to warm ourselves. For a while it worked. We did multiply and subdue the Earth. Our children will credit us for that, but they must face the fact that the Earth is not theirs to subdue, but rather to cherish. There is only one Earth.

The solution is simple: We must go back to the world's ravaged places and bind up the wounds we've inflicted. We must do our best to restore the natural world to something like it was 200 years ago, before we monkeywrenched nature. We must redesign our cities at the same time. Otherwise, we are out of here.

I believe this to be the most important challenge we face on Earth. Old, tired, me-first thinking won't do it. There is still time for the contrivers in America to come up with a better answer before the harm becomes irreparable.

WHILE I WAS WRITING this book, I attended my first Grateful Dead concert. I was invited by Dead musician Bob Weir, who had attended my eighty-second birthday party. The first thing I thought as I surveyed the crowd of 22,000 swaying twenty-four-year-olds was that my presence would bring the average age up to at least twenty-four and a half.

Then I wondered what wilderness experience would be left for these young people. What sort of a planet were we—members of my generation, and those quavering kids in their fifties and sixties, too—bequeathing? I thought of what I would say to these people if I could play Grateful Dead piano instead of semi-classical. What sort of speech might I give? It would have to be a short one. Maybe I would begin:

"While you are listening to this wonderful music that crosses so many boundaries, we are getting rid of the things worth crossing boundaries for. One of the most important things left on the

Earth for you is wilderness. Your minds, your bodies, the 100,000 chemical reactions that go on inside you without your knowing, the ability to hear the Dead in stereo, all were formed in wilderness, during the 4 billion years of life on this Earth: not in so-called civilization, not in the last two hundred years since the Industrial Revolution, but in wilderness. There have been no mistakes. You are here.

"There are things you can do to make life better," I would say, "to fix the Earth. If you don't do it, it won't get done. That wilderness within you and without you won't be there." Maybe there'd be a little foot shuffling at this point, so I'd remind them, "Hey, I'm an elder. You've got to listen to me. It took me a long time to become one. It won't take you that long. I'm sorry to give you the bad news, but you're going to be as old as I am much sooner than you think."

If that didn't get a laugh, I'd say, "I know, there's this problem with the environmental movement. It's like the problem of the Bible. There's no humor in it. I would say, Whatever you do, don't violate Rule Number 6. What is Rule Number 6? Rule Number 6 says, Never take yourself too seriously. (Of course, I do, but I pretend I don't.) What are the other rules? There are no other rules."

Most of these young people were probably gainfully employed. I would say to them, "Put some eco-spin into your job description—whatever you do in life, make sure to include CPR for the Earth. The Earth is a living throbbing organism. It needs CPR—Conservation-Preservation-Restoration—on a regular basis:

"*Conservation:* We've got to use our resources rationally. We haven't been all that rational these last brief millennia.

"*Preservation:* We've got to preserve what we can never replace. That's what wilderness is. That's what biodiversity is, and we're getting rid of both faster than anybody has ever done.

"*Restoration:* We're bright enough to build back, to restore the rivers we've dammed, the forests we've clearcut, the seas we've bloodied, polluted, and strip-mined with drift nets; the mountains we've bolted and bulldozed, the deserts we've spoiled or mistakenly created; the ozone layer we've punctured. We can't restore a lot of things that are gone, but we can certainly restore human integrity."

That's a little heavy. I wouldn't want to lose my audience. I would quickly add, "You have opportunities. Seize them."

Then I might think, Maybe these young people have never even seen a wilderness the way I have been privileged to, countless times. So I would add, "If this amphitheater were a wilderness and you were all here, it wouldn't be a wilderness anymore. Just a few of you should come to the wilderness at one time. And bring your music. Not just to listen, but to create some yourself. Learn to hear the music of the Earth."

Maybe someone heckles me: "Music like what!"

"Like the sound of a small stream," I would reply. "Like a canyon wren trilling down the scale in counterpoint. Dam that stream? It's your choice. Quell that bird, if you dare. But ask yourself what your grandchildren will ask you: What was it like, that *music*?"

I would still be tempted to tell them about a few of my own favorite places, but I would have to say, "This information is classified. If you want to know more about the places I really like to go, let's go out and close a bar."

After the Dead are done, of course.

THAT WAS my fantasy. In real life, Bob Weir came up to me backstage and asked where he could get my sweatshirt, which said across the chest: "Free Al Gore." Bob told me that he was a friend of the vice president, and would be meeting with him in a couple of weeks.

"You've got it," I said.

I liked Al Gore, I thought *Earth In the Balance* was one of the best books written by someone close to the American presidency since Theodore Roosevelt lost his comeback as leader of the Bull Moose Party. There are some things I disagree with in that book, but certainly a thinking man with children and heart wrote it.

One of the biggest disappointments of my life is that the movements to conserve, preserve, and restore the Earth is so absent from the legislative and political arena, which is like trying to walk in a wheelchair. The speed with which we are losing the Earth is devastating, and must be reversed, fast. We supporters of the environmental movement need to support the U-turn.

What I want to know is, did Al Gore get my sweatshirt and wear it to a cabinet meeting or photo opportunity? If he did, maybe things will change a little. Rule Number 6, remember.

IN THIS BOOK, let me share with you some visions of how we can make our children proud of the paradise they will inherit. Let's remember how the Earth looked just a few hundred years ago, and let's talk about how our Earth ought to look in another hundred or so years from now. Let's talk about pelicans and tigers, bristlecone pines and hypercars, mountains and CPR for the Earth.

It will be an adventure to share together.

PART I

Opportunities

CHAPTER I

Seeing and Remembering

We are confronted with insurmountable opportunities.
—Pogo

MY FRIEND Ansel Adams, the photographer of Yosemite, said, "If you're going to get old, get as old as you can get." A few years ago, when I was seventy-seven, I asked To Whom It May Concern for a twenty-year extension. To quote George Burns, in whose reckoning I must have been a teenager, "Shoot for 100. Very few people die after that." I say, borrow time without compunction: There is plenty of time later to be dead.

When you're my age, you think you're an oracle and that people had better listen to you. In fact, they sometimes seem to like to.

Life can begin at eighty, but you don't need to wait that long.

MY EARLIER LIFE began in 1912 beside the tracks of the Atcheson, Topeka, and Santa Fe in Berkeley, California. My earliest memory is of my brother, three years old, standing in his bed, silhouetted against the headlight of an oncoming railroad loco-motive as it roared past our bedroom. I was six months old. Whoever doesn't believe this is invited to disprove it.

When I was nine, in 1921, I remember traveling in a Maxwell touring car up the old one-lane dirt road to Lake Tahoe, in the Sierra. It took three days to get there. We camped well be-yond Colfax, in a forest of mixed pine and fir. Right away, I went exploring and I found a spring. I knew what a spring was because my father, an instructor of descriptive geometry at the Univer-sity of California, had shown me one in the hills behind campus, not far beyond where the first cyclotron would later be built. I was quite pleased to find clear water bubbling from dirt.

The next summer we drove back up to Tahoe and over to Donner Lake, where the early immigrants had met such misfor-tune, and we stopped at the same campsite where I had discov-ered the spring. It was gone. The forest all around it was gone.

Two years before that Sierra spring was clearcut, I became the eyes for my mother. She had lost her sight right after the birth of my younger brother. The cause was an inoperable brain tumor. When she regained her strength, she was first guided on a walk of two blocks to church. Then she got bold, and I got bold, and together we walked from our house, about 200 feet above sea level, to Grizzly Peak—at 1,759 feet, it was the second-highest point in our Berkeley Hills.

It was a joyful thing, that first big walk. It was my job to tell my mother where to put her feet in the rough places, and which one, right or left, but there was no great worry. She was a country girl, my mother, in her early forties and strong. She liked to be outdoors. Even blind, she felt good about it. At the top, I described the vista for her: the hills; the galaxy of flowers; the few new houses; a red-tailed hawk floating on the wind, looking for field mice; the fog coming over San Francisco Bay; the glimpse of the open sea through the Golden Gate. There was no Golden Gate Bridge, no Bay Bridge, so many fewer people in San Francisco, Oakland, San Jose, and Marin. We didn't have all the gas-powered vehicles then. We hadn't manufactured all that smog.

I THINK NOW that those loggers who destroyed my spring, and the Forest Service that served them, went about their work with the same dedication as a whaler hunting down the last blue whale. It was their livelihood, those loggers, their lifestyle, their art. But it is *our* future.

I think too about all the wild beauty I saw for my mother, and the destruction of that beauty that I've seen for myself. When this unsustainable orgy of cutting and running is finally over, the logger, like the buffalo hunter, like the whaler, will exist only in storybooks. I believe it will come true, and in your lifetime.

It would be too easy, however, to blame the destruction of the Earth's forests on those men who logged my cherished spring, or on a few misguided scientists. We have all played a role by belonging to a society that judges its worth by the quantity of what it consumes. By not remembering, by refusing to see.

I have seen a lot go right in my eighty-seven years on the planet, but I've also seen a lot go wrong. In my lifetime the world has used up four times the resources it used in all previous history. The population of the Earth has tripled, to what some ecologists think is about ten times the number the planet is capable of sustaining, given what we have chewed up so far. By 2010 it is expected to double again. Humans are far too fertile and over-consuming, especially in the North. Good breeding has been overdone.

Since that moment when I stood describing for my mother the view over the waters of San Francisco Bay, we've lost more than half of our native redwoods. Only 4 percent of the original stand is left. Some remain in Muir Woods, just below Mount Tamalpais, across the bay from where we stood. There used to be 6,000 miles of good salmon streams in California's Central Valley. Now we're down to about 200, and people are arguing over how much water the endangered salmon should be allowed to be endangered in. Only eighty years ago there were no dams on the mighty Columbia River. Now there are many dams, and the salmon don't like it.

There are too many dams on the Snake River, as well as on the Frazier, the Sacramento, and the San Joaquin. There's just a piddling left for those salmon, and those that make it over the fish ladders to spawn. Once they hatch, the few young salmon must then swim miles through slack water, survive turbines, and, if they make it to the ocean, they must contend with drift-netters on the high seas—the buffalo hunters of our time.

As for the inexhaustible sacred cod of the Grand Banks, they are all but gone. Imagine. It has taken five centuries, but they have become like the passenger pigeon. Forty to one hundred species of plant or animal life disappear every day—nobody knows how many for sure.

As entire mosaics of green ecosystems disappear, so, too, do the birds—three decades after Rachel Carson wrote *Silent Spring*. We won some good battles on behalf of the eagle and the peregrine, but the DDT that once weakened the shells of their eggs is still cheaply available in developing countries. Seventy percent of the bird species in the world are in decline, and about 1,000 face extinction.

As the protective ozone layer of our planet thins, we suspect that the increased radiation is killing off toads and frogs in America's Sierra and Cascades. In Australia, billboards proclaim the danger to fair-skinned humans; and cats, whose sunburned ears have been removed in hopes that skin cancer will not metastasize, sadly walk Australia's gardens and streets.

In Florida, alligators are born with small and malformed penises. In Britain, male trout, under the mistaken hormonal impression that they are females, are producing albumen for eggs they will never form. The industrialized world is awash in a sea of estrogens. These estrogens, most chemically derived, are believed to originate in certain plastics and from the pollution of our clean water, and the implications are not good for the males of our own species, who have in the United States experienced a twofold increase in prostate cancer in recent decades; Denmark and other European countries have seen a threefold increase in cancer of the testes.

When I was a boy, water was cleaner. It should be more so now. But you can't purify water with additives.

What happened? Sometimes we have been greedy and un-thinking, but at other times the road to environmental disaster has been paved with good intentions. Too often in what we do, we fail to consider the two most important things: the cost to the future, and the cost to the Earth. We can be very clever, we humans, but sometimes not so smart.

In Egypt, the Nile River had been doing just fine for millennia, annually flooding its banks with life-giving nutrients, which made early agriculture possible and later fed an immense sardine fishery in the Mediterranean. Then Russia rushed to help dam the Nile at Aswân, to provide hydroelectric power. In my lifetime no more crazy things have been done than in the mad dash for more energy, and the way we use it. These days, the sardines in the Mediterranean are dead and gone, and Egypt's farmers are not so happy, either. Now the Nile offers not good soil but crop-weakening salts. In some of the new warm irrigation ditches, a parasite that lives in the snails has infected three-quarters of the human population with schistosomiasis, and it is not a nice disease.

In America, we stopped man's hubris in the Grand Canyon of the Colorado River, one of the planet's most sublime chasms. There the battle was fought and won in the name of Beauty. They wanted to dam the waters.

I was then the first executive director of the Sierra Club. We put full-page ads in the *New York Times, Washington Post,* and other papers and magazines. One of my favorites ran in *Scientific American* and asked: "Should We Also Flood the Sistine Chapel So Tourists Can Get Nearer the Ceiling?" The ads—augmented by strenuous lobbying, thousands of letters and phone calls, two books, and two films—helped kill the dam. One ad also ended the tax-deductible status of the Sierra Club. In fact, the U.S. Internal Revenue Service, which may have been less subtle in those days, ended our eco-innocence (tax-deductible income) that very day, when the director of the IRS met over drinks with one angry and powerful congressman, who later became a friend of mine.

In the twenty-five years since the first Earth Day, that magnificent outpouring of awareness, we have reduced enough forests around the world to cover the United States from the Mississippi to the Atlantic seaboard, north to south. We've created enough desert to equal all the cropland in China. We've lost enough soil by other means—pavement and condominiums, wind and water erosion, inundation, and poorly informed application of chemicals—to equal all the cropland in India. That's one-seventh of the world's productive land lost since Earth Day began. And in that time our population doubled.

The enormity of what we are doing must come to pervade our thinking. Our religions haven't quite prepared us for our current situation.

I was once at a conference where the aim was to expose Presbyterians to an environmentalist. A minister said Man was co-creator, with God, of the Earth. Anybody who thinks he is a co-creator with God is having a little trouble with humility. Why would God pick something that came along so very recently to be in His image? I realized we were probably the most arrogant species that had ever arrived on Earth, as well as the Johnny-come-latelies of evolution. It occurred to me then that should we squeeze the age of the Earth down to six days of biblical creation, we would get a time line something like this (and not a few people have repeated my thought):

Sunday at midnight, the Earth is created. There is no life until Tuesday noon. Millions upon millions of species come during the week, and millions of species go. By Saturday morning at seven, there's been enough chlorophyll manufactured for the fossil fuels to begin to form. Around four in the afternoon, the great reptiles come on stage. They hang around for a long time, as species go, until nine-thirty, a five-hour run. The Grand Canyon begins taking shape eighteen minutes before midnight. Nothing like us shows up for another fifteen minutes. No Homo sapiens until thirty seconds ago. Let the party begin! A second and a half back, we throw the habits of hunting and gathering to the winds, and learn to change the environment to suit our appetites. We get rid of everything we can't eat as fast as we possibly can, and that's the beginning of agriculture.

A third of a second before midnight, Buddha; a quarter of a second, Jesus Christ; a fortieth of a second, the Industrial Revolution; an eightieth of a second, we discover oil; a two-hundredth of a second, how to split atoms. What we haven't discovered, even now, is how to leave hubris at the door. There's still an overdose of pride in our species. As Voltaire said, "Man learned the art of speech so that his meaning could be hidden."

Once we learned the art of speech, we stopped understanding each other.

AS BIOLOGIST E. O. Wilson of Harvard University points out, we are the first species to grasp the existence of the universe, the biosphere, the whole works. Yet even though we comprehend, we are still doing everything we can to get rid of it. We've picked up some bad habits in the last 500,000 years. As thinking people, as environmentalists, all we have been able to do is to slow down the rate at which things have been getting worse.

I, however, am an optimist. I agree with Pogo, that wise cartoon character from my late middle age, who said, "We have met the enemy and he is us." But I also agree with what Pogo added sometime later: "We are confronted with insurmountable opportunities." In my day, when someone proclaimed a mountain to be insurmountable, it was climbed within a year.

CHAPTER 2

Climbing Mountains

Only the mountain has lived long enough to listen
objectively to the howl of the wolf.

—Aldo Leopold, "Thinking Like a Mountain"

I USED TO BE a mountaineer, and I still enjoy the
company of mountaineers. I never got over my love of climbing, that process by which you and the rock are learning what
you can do with each other.

They credit me with seventy first ascents. Most exhilarating
was the first ascent of Shiprock, on the Navajo Reservation in the
Southwestern United States. Shiprock is tall and jagged, a former
volcanic neck made of rhyolitic breccia that rises 1,500 feet above
the desert floor. From a distance it looks like a windjammer in full
sail. By 1939, when I was twenty-seven, Shiprock had become the
leading challenge to climbers in the United States. Party after
party had attempted its crumbling walls and concluded that the
formation could not be climbed. Bestor Robinson, Raffi Bedayan,

John Dyer, and I were young enough and cocky enough to make another pass at the peak, but with some technological help: expansion bolts, which had never before been used to anchor the belays required in technical mountaineering, and pitons.

We drove our pitons—spikes made of iron or good steel—into cracks that already existed in the rock. If it is the right size crack and the right size piton, it goes in and jams quite well. You've got to have the correct steel so that it can take a little bit of distortion in its shape to accommodate the rock, in order to help make the seal.

Before we drove to the desert, we studied every photograph we could get. We wanted to figure the weaknesses in the mountain's defense. Everybody before us had tried to go all the way up Shiprock's west side. This was understandable, because that was where the only sound rock on the mountain was, a vertical dike of basalt. It's more fun to climb a mountain that's willing to hold itself together, rather than one you have to hold together as you climb it.

From the pictures, we got the idea of proceeding up the dike to the base of the north tower, then fixing a rope and rappelling down a chute, and traversing to the east side and the base of the main tower.

We put the first two expansion bolts to be used in mountaineering at the base of a double overhang, the most challenging pitch of the climb. It's hard to get used to walking on air. Johnny Dyer led it because he was the lightest member of the party, and we could more easily hold him if he fell. Were he not protected by our belays, he could have had a bit of a tumble—about 1,000 feet. Johnny led the two very tough pitches where there was a heavy likelihood of falling, and I led the rest. We wore old-fashioned crepe-soled basketball shoes and exercised a lot of caution. We held group conferences on lofty ledges, spent a restless third night hanging out with the lizards, and finally I was able to yodel victoriously from the narrow topmast that only circling crows had landed on before.

I like to test things. I used to drive a lot of pitons and take them out and look at them to see how well they did. We initiated the use of those expansion bolts. The expansion bolts and pitons made our ascent possible, and they probably saved our lives. Unfortunately, they also damaged the mountain.

THE PROBLEM with all technology, from expansion bolts to nuclear power plants, is that it must be used to correct the errors it invites. Happily, it's easier to take a piton out of a crack than to dismantle a nuclear power plant along the California coast. I have been called a druid often enough, even an archdruid. I don't want to see rampant technology drive the world into going Luddite, destroying technology in the name of preservation; and I still admire scientists, but not when they substitute arrogance for science. I particularly enjoy asking scientists which of their firm beliefs of today they think are most likely to be laughed at in twenty-five years.

I wish that everyone who seeks to lead the environmental cause could experience the peak moments of a climb. There is a lot to be learned from climbing mountains, more than you might think, about life, about saving the Earth, and not a little about how to go about both. Tough mountains build bold leaders, many of whom, in the early days, came down from the mountains to save them. The world now needs these leaders—people willing to take a chance—as it has never needed them before.

John Muir's readers are well aware of his boldness as a mountaineer and wilderness adventurer, whether from his accounts of his ascent of Mount Ritter, his traverse on the narrow ledge under Upper Yosemite Fall, his climb to the top of a storm-tossed tree, or his perils on a glacier in Alaska with his dog Stickeen. Muir was also a bold leader of the Sierra Club. The early leaders of the Sierra Club gained daring from their exploration of Sierra Nevada summits and routes, and seven have had summits named after them. None of them hired guides to lead them. They learned from each other and from the mountains.

What did they learn?

Judgment, for one thing. Climbers with poor judgment can expect to be weeded out early. Whether you climb a mountain for exercise, for challenge, for perspective, "because it's there," or because it's up and you like to keep on top of things, you start out by making judgments.

When you want to get to the top, you need to decide how to avoid the barriers along the way. You take along enough human support and technical protection to give you a chance to fall more than once. You select the best possible route from far enough away so you know where the dead ends are and where you don't want to be if rock or ice decides to fall. You take with you enough training to know your physical limits. You don't expose yourself to more weather than you can handle, and you dress for the worst you can reasonably expect. In the back of your mind you remember that the mountain will be there tomorrow if today it refuses to cooperate. And if your sport is roped climbing, you know that a special kind of love travels both ways along that rope.

You take risks. You search. Sometimes luck is with you, and sometimes not, but the important thing is to take the dare. A new fact has recently become clear to me: It is not variety that is the spice of life. Variety is the meat and potatoes. Risk is the spice of life. Those who climb mountains or raft rivers understand this.

WHAT HAS HAPPENED to boldness in defense of the Earth? For all the splendid increase in membership of the world's environmental organizations, both wilderness and the ecological life-support system of the planet itself are increasingly going down the tubes. Could this be because large environmental groups are acting like government bureaucracies? Consider what my friend Justice William O. Douglas once told President Franklin Delano Roosevelt: Any government bureau more than ten years old should be abolished, because after that it becomes more concerned with its image than with its mission.

In the United States, the environmental movement has saved millions of acres of wilderness, thousands of acres of ancient forests, and rare deserts—saved them for future generations to keep on saving. But for every acre preserved, several have been lost.

Compromise is often necessary, but it ought not to originate with environmental leaders. Our role is to hold fast to what we believe is right, to fight for it, to find allies, and to adduce all possible arguments for our cause. If we cannot find enough vigor in us or our friends to win, then let someone else propose the compromise, which we must then work hard to coax our way. We thus become a nucleus around which activists can build and function.

When the U.S. government proposed dams for the Grand Canyon, we at the Sierra Club said we'd accept no dams. People knew what we stood for and gathered around. We defeated the proposals. If we had said (or thought) that we'd accept one dam but not two, clarity would have vanished from our deeds and faces. People would have seen that we were just arguing about how much defilement is acceptable, not opposing it entirely. They would have gathered elsewhere if they gathered at all. Too often, in the 1990s, environmentalists are so eager to appear reasonable that they have gone soft.

Russell Train, the principal environmental adviser to Richard Nixon, that most contradictory of our "environmental presidents," once said of me, "Thank God for David Brower. He makes it so easy for the rest of us to be reasonable."

I WAS NOT ALWAYS unreasonable, and I am sorry for that. By being just a bit less reasonable, I could have stopped the construction of Glen Canyon Dam, which flooded the last large roadless area between Canada and Mexico, and supplanted it with mechanical recreation areas.

My first victory as executive director of the Sierra Club was helping to stop two dams in Dinosaur National Monument, straddling the Utah-Colorado border. I always like to say, the way to instill youthful confidence and avoid octogenarian burnout is to enjoy at least one consecutive success. We had a few more successes along the way—Point Reyes National Seashore, Fire Island, Cape Cod, Redwood National Park, North Cascades, the national wilderness system—some big wins. I knew what all of these areas looked like. I had been there—rafting the rivers, exploring the canyons, drinking from the springs that cascade out of the high desert walls, some as high as two or three thousand feet. But I had never seen Glen Canyon. I was as blind toward it as my mother, yet, I am sorry to say, without her vision.

I was sitting in the House Gallery, in Washington, D.C., and we had 200 votes to stop the entire Colorado River project. But earlier that day I had received a telegram informing me that the board of our organization had decided to make a compromise. If two dams, Echo Park and Split Mountain, were taken out of the total project, we would withdraw our opposition.

I did not do what a leader should have done, which was hop the next plane to the West Coast and rally the board to righteousness. Instead, I sat on my duff. Now, believe me, the Bureau of Reclamation did not need this dam. It would irrigate nothing. Into the twenty-second century, if then, city dwellers in the region will not need that "placid evaporation tank," as Edward Abbey once described another boondoggle impoundment. Instead, I was uncharacteristically reasonable. I compromised. Now I have to live with that, the flooding of the place no one knew, Glen Canyon. But only until we drain Lake Powell.

This is how in 1869 that one-armed explorer, John Wesley Powell, described the canyon none of us will ever see again:

> Past these towering monuments, past these mounded
> billows of ornate sandstone, past these oak-set glens, past
> these fern-decked alcoves, past these mural curves, we
> glide hour after hour, stopping now and then, as our
> attention is arrested by some new wonder.

I say to all who consider themselves to be the friends of the Earth, and especially to those of you who consider yourselves leaders: Never give up what you haven't seen (unless they be chlorofluorocarbons). And don't expect politicians, even good ones, to do the job for you. Politicians are like weather vanes. Our job is to make the wind blow.

CHAPTER 3

The Bristlecone Pine

Leave it as it is. The ages have been at work on it,
and man can only mar it.

—Theodore Roosevelt

IN NATURE, making the wind blow can be a mistake.
I know, because I tried it.

When I was eleven, I had the idea of raising butterflies. I
liked western swallowtails, which are exquisite creatures, about
three inches in wingspan, yellow with a black border. Just above
the tail they have eye spots of a rainbow hue. My neighborhood
had many swallowtails, and was full of anise—ample butterfly
food. I started with the eggs. Tiny caterpillars emerged, yellow-
banded squibs of black. The caterpillars later turned green and
then into chrysalides. I waited.

When the day came, the first chrysalid cracked. An antenna
popped out. Another. Then the butterfly laboriously climbed
out. The abdomen was extended, full of fluid that was pumped
into the unexpanded wings as the butterfly clung upside down

on a twig. Thirty minutes later, the former caterpillar was aloft. A miracle—which was about to be short-circuited in my desire to help what I did not understand.

As the remaining chrysalides split, I lent a finger. Very gently, I widened their cracking skins. The creatures promptly emerged. They just crawled about. What had been genetically designed had been undone. What was supposed to happen now could not. The flow of fluid was not triggered by the butterflies' own exertions and failed to reach the wings. They all died. I had tried to free them, and by freeing them I had killed them.

WHEN WE WERE fighting to establish a new Redwood National Park, I learned an amazing fact about redwoods. When a 500-year flood deposited deep sediment over the roots, new roots emerged at the right new level, having to punch their way through several inches of bark. Somehow the trees knew how, when, and where to do that. I was freshly impressed with the information that is packed into a redwood seed.

I was also impressed on the roof of a New Yorker's penthouse, seventy stories about asphalt, by a great tree in a small tub producing apples. How does the tree do that? There is a little bit of magic in that tub, and that magic is called soil. To put it teleologically, I like to say: Trees were invented by the soil so it wouldn't have to move.

AS I WAS FOUNDING Friends of the Earth, which is now in sixty-five countries, I suddenly realized that I had never wanted anybody to tell me what to do. I just wanted to coax other people. Respecting the creativity within other people is a hard business to get into.

It occurred to me then that we are like the seeds of the bristlecone pine. Bristlecones grow in the high desert ranges of California and Nevada. On the windward side of White Mountain Peak in California, centuries of wind have stripped their soil away, leaving old roots hanging in the air. The bristlecone pine is the oldest living tree on Earth. The very oldest one we know of was 5,000 years old, and was cut down so a scientist could count the rings.

We don't have to tell the seeds of the bristlecone pine what to do. We give them a chance. Or God does. Or Whom It May Concern does. Now, I'm not about to tell a bristlecone pine, or for that matter, a western swallowtail, a condor, or a redwood, what to do. I've learned my lesson well. They know, I am quite willing to ask the rest of us not to stop bristlecones from growing. We have no right to drive these miracles off the Earth.

As my friend Bernadette Cozart, who is restoring gardens and wildness to Harlem, says, "Sometimes I think we must be the youngest species on Earth, because everything else seems to know what to do."

CHAPTER 4

Visions of a Wild Century

What will it say about the human race if we let the tiger
go extinct? What can we save? Can we save ourselves?
—Ashok Kumar

LET ME TELL YOU the sad tale of two wild creatures
that you might think have nothing in common: the tiger and
the dolphin. One has fur, the other has fins. One roams the land,
the other the sea. But for both of them, survival is up for grabs.

Outside a shop in Taiwan, a live tiger is staked upside down
inside a cage, legs tethered, head outside the bars. An auction is
going on, and buyers and bystanders alike appraise the imagined
virility of this animal. In the wild tigers may make love several
times an hour, if their mates happen to be in estrus. Some of the
buyers at the shop's auction have flagging libidos, or at least their
customers do, and they all hope that the tiger's vigor will somehow translate to them through the medium of tiger penis soup,
which can cost $320 a bowl. Other customers believe tiger bone
cures rheumatism, or that tiger whiskers impart strength, or that

tiger eye stops certain types of convulsions. The various parts of this dead tiger may bring a retailer as much as $60,000. The auction is soon over. The tiger's throat is slit, and the organs and bone, the penis and pelt, are parceled out to the highest bidders.

Off the coast of Costa Rica, the *Maria Luisa*, a tuna fishing boat, sets its net around a school of disporting dolphins. In the eastern tropical Pacific, the presence of dolphins often indicates yellowfin tuna under the surface. A mechanical winch pulls up the net, and a dolphin is snagged by its dorsal fin and raised high above the ship. The dolphin writhes and twists. The dorsal fin tears off. The net is pulled aboard, as more dolphins are being maimed and drowned. The crew, intent on the tuna catch, rip the mammals from the net. Some are already dead; others still struggle as they are thrown into a chute and dumped overboard as *comida para los tiburones*, "food for the sharks." This day, almost 200 dolphins have been rendered into shark food in the process of catching only twelve yellowfin tuna, a worse than normal ratio. These dolphins happen to be endangered Costa Rican spinners. In the middle of the eastern Pacific, the same story is being played out. The fishermen lay out their huge nets. The noose closes. The tuna are hauled aboard, and with them the dolphins, whose meat few wish to eat. The dolphins are cut from the net, and tossed into the shark chute.

WE KNOW ABOUT the tiger and the dolphin because of the work of biologist Sam LaBudde. Posing as a deckhand on one of those tuna boats, he brought a video camera on board and shot the footage under the guise of making a home movie. He also took pictures of that tiger, and of what happened to it. Decades ago, when our task was to convince people of the need to create national parks and seashores, to preserve wilderness areas, and to save the Grand Canyon, I aimed my 16-millimeter Bell and Howell at Yosemite Valley, at Hetch Hetchy, at a sunset ascent of North Palisade, the highest peak in what was not yet Kings Canyon National Park. When these films were played, people understood what was about to be destroyed, and at their expense. Sam LaBudde knew that eyewitness evidence was still the best.

There are only about 5,000 to 7,500 tigers lift in the world, fewer now than when I first wrote this, and about one-twentieth the number that existed at the turn of the century. Seven to ten million dolphins, many representing three-quarters of one species, had been terminated from the eastern Pacific before Sam began to ask the obvious questions: Who is making money from this carnage? How can we let people know what is going on? Should we care?

Sam LaBudde is an intense young man. When he got off the *Maria Luisa* in 1988, he learned to communicate in six- to eight- second sound bites. He learned to tell people what he had seen in ways that would be effective. But he was still stumped by that third question, Why should we care? He says, "It was like when you walk around in high school or college late at night by yourself or with a friend and try to figure out what truth is, or if there really is a God. I was trying to work out how to make dolphins mean something to all of us. Finally, it occurred to me: Dolphins are the only wild species on the planet that values human life."

When Sam was a machinist in Alaska, people would bring him broken, tortured, and mangled machinery. Sam's job was to make the parts whole again. Every day he learned how to get from Point A to Point B—how to get the job done. He believes that too many environmentalists are process driven these days. As far as being an environmentalist goes, he says, repairing machinery is the most valuable job he could have had. We have to set goals and get the job done.

Sam sits down with a pencil and paper and thinks through the problem: "Tuna sometimes travel with dolphins. Tuna nets kill dolphins. U.S. law allows it (or did). The public does not know the simple truth, that tuna fish sandwiches can cause dolphins to be killed in purse seines. People buy tuna, and essentially pay the fishermen—the tuna canning companies—to go out and kill more dolphins."

In their dolphin campaign, Sam and Earth Island Institute threw up as many roadblocks as they could: emotional, political, legislative, media, consumer, and legal. If they could cut the "circle of destruction" at any point, the whole cycle would stop.

Ultimately, Sam zeroed in on the weakest link in the food chain, which in this case was you and me, and our taste for the little tin cans of tuna sold by H. J. Heinz and other tuna companies. The Heinz people had spent decades creating a wholesome ma-and-pa image for their products, from baby food to dog food. When Sam's video images of what was going on behind the scenes hit the media—and they hit like a freight train—H. J. Heinz realized it could not afford to be characterized as a dolphin-killing company. The stockholders didn't like it much either, and the children of the executives and directors were mostly appalled. The truth about tuna and dolphins even permeated Hollywood. In the movie *Lethal Weapon*, Danny Glover, as a police officer, fixes himself tuna with mayo on white bread. His child stops him: "Dad, don't eat that tuna. You're killing dolphins."

The final blow came when LaBudde organized activists in two dozen major U.S. cities to target Heinz with simultaneous demonstrations a week before the twentieth anniversary of Earth Day. "National Dolphin Day" was to be the day that changed Heinz from a welcome guest in the nation's pantries into "the dolphin-killing company." Instead, Heinz dodged the bullet by convening a press conference in Washington, D.C., forty-eight hours beforehand, and announcing it would no longer buy tuna caught by killing dolphins. Most other U.S. tuna canners quickly followed. National Dolphin Day turned into a celebration.

This was certainly one of the most precipitous changes in consumer buying habits ever to come about, and it all goes back to the pictures, to Sam's courageous use of video. "The visual truth of a situation can move millions of people," he says, "and their outcry moves politicians and bureaucrats. Without visual ammunition we are like unarmed soldiers marching into battle."

Photographs of staked tigers, video of skeletons dumped from bags and reassembled on dirt floors, eerie shots of skinned skulls, and also of fine, finished tiger skins packaged for jaded collectors in the Middle East and elsewhere, all have become the visual ammunition in the battle to save the world's endangered tigers. People have been moved.

But as with dolphins, the causal engine driving the equation is the market, the illegal international trade in tiger parts. It has also played a part in the demise of the African elephant, the rhino, the leopard, scores of beautiful birds such as the scarlet macaw, and even bears from many places in the world. At the turn of the century, the world supported over 1 million rhinos. Now there are fewer than 10,000. Africa and India once had 10 million elephants. Now there are about 600,000.

Incredibly, the illegal trade in bear gall, live birds, leopard skin, rhino horn, tiger bone, ivory, and other wildlife represents the third most lucrative form of international crime, after drugs and gun smuggling. Sam believes the revenue from this macabre commerce is in excess of $2 billion annually. This does not count the cost of interdiction, nor the cost to the economies of the concerned countries. It certainly does not count the cost to the Earth or the tiger. And who would fly to Kenya for a photo safari when the rhinos have been machine-gunned?

ONCE LABUDDE and others around the world put out the visual ammunition concerning the tiger trade, sympathetic governments had the proof they needed to take action against outlaw countries. In 1994 the United Nations-sponsored Convention on International Trade in Endangered Species (CITES) recommended that international trade sanctions be levied against Taiwan for condoning and allowing the commerce. This means that the United

States and other countries that were members of CITES could impose trade sanctions against products coming from Taiwan. That has real economic and political clout. It curbs foul appetites.

The goal of these campaigns is to save the animal. All along, environmentalists must keep asking: How many dolphins have we saved? How many tigers? The amount of money raised, the size of an activist organization, everything else must be subordinated to that question. The Earth demands an honest answer.

Some things must be done now, such as saving the big cats. There is no tomorrow for them unless we insure it today. Other things take time. Restoring habitat, the fragile web that sustains a climax predator such as the tiger, takes a great deal of time. We need to get off our duffs and start now, but we must keep an effort going for fifty, one hundred, even two hundred years, if we wish truly to restore wonders like the tiger habitat, the Everglades in Florida, or the tall grass prairie of the United States, where the buffalo once roamed.

Sam LaBudde says, "You can't promote habitat protection. It's not sexy enough. You've got to use a species as a charismatic symbol. . . . The only international habitat campaign that sells is the rain forest, because it's intriguing. If you shout, 'Save the tall grass prairie!' everybody yawns. They ask, 'What's on the other channel?' Now if you like saving bison . . . "

Of course, Sam is a little young and tough, new school. Well, maybe Sam's right about the need for a "sexy animal" to catch people's interest. But I don't yawn when you say "tall grass prairie." It teaches you what grass roots are all about.

PART II

Solutions

CHAPTER 5

Havens

The greatest beauty is organic wholeness
The divine beauty of the universe . . .
Love that, not man apart . . .
  —Robinson Jeffers

RARE CREATURES such as wolves, grizzlies, buffalo, trumpeter swans, giant sequoias, and the bristlecone pines still thrive in the special places we began setting aside for them more than a century ago. A new kind of foresight brought us Yosemite and Yellowstone. This was John Muir's legacy, the American conservation movement. Large blocks of essentially primeval forest and land were put aside in the Adirondacks of New York, to be forever wild. Later, some vast reaches of essential habitat were protected through the Wilderness System.

Unfortunately, too much of what civilization has saved as wilderness has been called "wilderness on the rocks"—to be saved, the land was required to be of low commercial value. Too much was not saved because cities and suburbs crept out from the edges while their centers decayed.

Thoreau asked long ago, "What's the use of a house if you haven't got a tolerable planet to put it it on?" We have been overly enamored of that house and of human beings. We have forgotten the context, without which neither is possible.

Still, we have a fair idea of the beauty that surrounded people a century ago. What do we want the place to look like, and be home to, a century hence?

By setting a goal now, we have a chance to restore what we can of what was needlessly and thoughtlessly lost.

I LIKE THE IDEA of aiming high. Navigators have been aiming at stars for ages. They haven't hit one yet, but they got where they wanted to get because they knew where to aim.

Because our ancestors aimed high, we have sanctuaries that help protect some of our most important species: grizzlies, spotted owls, the marbled murrelet, wolves, and wolverines (the only mammal, Olaus Murie once told me, that doesn't get arthritis). These species are often the best indicators of habitat health. Many biologists call these sanctuaries core reserves. I'd rather call them havens.

All over the Earth there are havens. Some of them even have tigers on them, running free (or as one writer dryly put it years ago, they have wildlife running around uncooked).

The havens are great, but they won't be enough in the long run. Here's what I think we need to do: We need to expand and extend these havens, then surround them with buffer zones that afford somewhat less protection, until we reach the fully developed areas—our cities of the future. These cities would need their own boundaries. Yes, we need boundaries around cities, not around wildness.

Animals and seeds do not honor the straight lines on human maps. They follow river beds, they migrate through mountain passes, they forage from mountain to plain, they pass from public forest to private, they blow where the wind blows. At least they used to.

If members of a particular species find themselves holed up on some island haven, even one as large as Yellowstone Park, for example, they may lose their wanderlust. Havens, even large ones, may not allow for genetic diversity. In addition, in times of stress—when prairies are too hot, or mountains run out of white pine nuts and tasty cutworms, which grizzlies love—then certain animals need to move along to greener pastures. If greener pastures are already occupied, the animals are out of luck.

So to link up these big protected core havens that we already possess to a certain extent in the United States, we would need to add a system of wildlife corridors. I call these corridors, *high ways*, not highways, as in interstates. I like to separate the words "high" and "way" in order to impart some of that original First Nation (or Indian) feeling to the routes that animals and some plants once traveled.

Whatever name you prefer, help it happen. My wife, Anne, and I were fascinated by the creative thinking we encountered in a Wild Earth conference at Sagamore, in the Adirondacks, in 1994. Some thirty-five experts spent three days marking up maps spread out all over the floor, and asking some exciting questions: Where should the cores, buffers, and corridors be between the Atlantic shore and the Great Lakes? Or from the Adirondacks north into the three adjoining provinces of Canada? Conference organizer Dave Foreman's enthusiasm for this kind of planning for the next fifty years was totally contagious. I can't wait to see the composite haven maps published in draft form and the general public asked to answer the question, "What did we forget?"

Plants and animals live in ecosystems, not parks, counties, states, or countries. By protecting havens and linking them with high ways, we would be trying to give fauna and flora what they had before we got here. Creatures live in a community of plants and animals that are recycled by sun, water, and soil.

Let's look at the northern Rockies bioregion as one example: the 18 million-acre Yellowstone ecosystem could be said to be bounded by the Wind, Salt, and Snake rivers to the south, the Yellowstone River to the north, the Clarks Fork to the east, and the valleys of the Gallatin and Madison to the west. In such an ecosystem, all beings, from wolf to lichen, can be seen to be linked. In order to protect the moose, the autotropic bacteria of Mammoth Hot Springs inside Yellowstone Park must also be protected, and with equal determination. The Florida Everglades, the Mojave Desert, and the Amazon are even bigger examples of ecosystems. Of course, an ecosystem can be as small as a rotting deer carcass or as large as the planet itself. Smaller systems are equally fascinating. E. O. Wilson tells us that there are 4,000 to 5,000 species of bacteria in one gram of Norwegian beach-forest soil, and this is glaciated earth. How many species frolic in a gram of soil that glaciers never edited?

LET'S PUT these ideas together: ecosystems, havens, buffer zones, and high ways or corridors.

Take the human-demarcated states of Idaho, Montana, and Wyoming, along with a little swatch of eastern Oregon and Washington, and a chunk of Alberta, in Canada (or let them take us). In this overview Yellowstone Park is a haven. So is Glacier-Waterton International Park. West of Yellowstone is another haven, the Salmon River region, one of the wildest spots in the country, where Marilyn Monroe and Robert Mitchum once filmed *River of No Return*. West of Glacier is a pristine group of forests, mountain ranges, and river valleys that biologists call the Greater Cabinet-Yaak-Selkirk.

On a map these wild areas resemble the four paw prints of a wolf, with the addition of the dewclaw of Greater Hell's Canyon, to the west of the Salmon. If there were high ways running among them, animals would be able to move back and forth in order to replenish their food and sexual stock, when necessary. We would have the beginnings of a restored ecosystem in this part of the northern Rockies.

I have used the northern Rockies as my example, rather than the Adirondacks, or the Southern Appalachians, or northern New England, because I have been quite active in the last couple of years in support of the Northern Rockies Ecosystem Protection Act. (Although the act has many supporters in the United States Congress, virtually none are from those states concerned. This was also the case, unfortunately, in our successful battles in Alaska.) Insiders' determination to exploit was outvoted by outsiders' hope to protect.

I believe that to protect biodiversity, we need to protect big chunks of linked wilderness. You can't do this in just one state, or even state by state. Politically, there is too much risk that the private interests, mining and logging, will chop us apart. They are better organized state by state than they are nationally, compared to environmentalists.

And what of us? We humans are part of the ecosystem, sometimes nicely so, sometimes not. Where, a century hence, might it be most useful for our grandchildren to be?

CHAPTER 6

Cities with Boundaries

What's the use of a house if you haven't got a tolerable
planet to put it on?

—Henry David Thoreau

AS PART of the struggle to save wilderness and Cree
territory in Quebec from Hydro-Quebec, I found myself and
the Cree chief driving into obsolescing northern Manhattan. A
brilliant old idea hit me: Why not give back the beads and offer
him Manhattan?

If New York City had contemplated drawing boundaries
around itself long ago, my idea might have had a chance. But New
York didn't, and my Cree friend had the right answer: "No way."

Cities worked very well, until they lost their main mission,
which was providing a proximity that allowed the gathering and
using of critical human talent and artifacts. Then the winds of
change blew their function away, and we ended up with less
urbia and too much sub. During the Middle Ages in Europe,

which I barely remember, cities had walls, models for our going back for the future and bringing it up to date. The peasant farmers of the Middle Ages worked fields outside the city walls. At night, or in times of trouble, they would retreat inside.

Now we've reversed that. Outside our cities lies a ring of suburbs, which have grown over the farms. You can make more money growing condominiums and malls than growing tomatoes. The inside of this un-magic circle, in places like West Oakland, the South Bronx, Albuquerque, or Rocinha, has been abandoned to the poorest people—mostly people of color—who soon become the unlucky ones chosen to receive our gifts of toxic waste dumps and incinerators.

It reminds me of fairy rings. In my decades of traveling on and off Sierra trails, I would come across these common rings of grass. The outside ring, ever expanding, was green and healthy—like new suburbs. Inside the ring—inner city—the grass was dead or dying, the nutrients used up.

Yet cities are essentially good. Without them you'd have to travel forever to find things. A healthy city is a concentration of human creativity, with all the exchanges of ideas and the nurturing of ethics. But they can develop by design, not by default. We've been draining the land around them until there are no farmers, only real estate speculation and, just beyond that, agribusiness. Agribusiness is not interested in farming, that is, in sustaining the soil. Agribusiness mines the soil, and tries its damnedest to addict the soil to chemicals that are disasters to it and, in the long term, to us. And soil, in the long run, is what sustains us.

Once upon a time, there really were cedars in Lebanon, and they existed in profusion. Nepal had more trees. Delhi, in the Central Valley of California, was thirty feet higher, before agribusiness mined the local aquifer, the water table dropped, and its roof collapsed.

In recommending that cities begin to cohere again, with boundaries that make ecological sense, I am not talking about the next few weeks, but the next few decades, the next few centuries.

There can be no slow solutions to fast problems, as Randall Hayes says. Nevertheless, in engineering long-term change, patience is important, lest fear scare off our natural allies. We have a large potential constituency: those who like to eat and breathe well.

Cities with boundaries will have to be creatively designed. We'll have to put a lot of thought into what our rational needs will be in 50 years, or 200 years. This is a fine challenge for architects, builders, engineers, bankers, artists, and all the rest of us. Cities ought not be structured by denial, simply to accommodate whatever the latest failure to think ahead may be. There will be less need for cars and timbered buildings, less junk mail, and less junk TV and the violence it has spawned. Many people have already begun to work at home. Let's encourage this. There really is no reason for suburbs. Cluster these migrant homes, offices, and shops, sometimes in the same building, with orchards on the roof.

Cities are necessary. They can be beautiful. But they need no longer be a plague upon the Earth.

I can't forget what the old city of Dubrovnik was—a World Cultural Heritage site—before the recent madness trashed it. No cars. The marble pavement polished by human feet, no horns sounding, just the almost lost music of friendly human voices.

CHAPTER 7

Eco-Preserves

His signature is the beauty of things.
—Robinson Jeffers

IS IT UNREASONABLE to imagine the Great Barrier Reef as one glorious, watery Earth Park? Lake Baikal and the forests of Siberia, a different sort of protected paradise? How about half of Tibet, the top of the world? The Dalai Lama likes the idea. It's his.

Shouldn't we all want the top of our world protected? Shouldn't these places, and more, be set aside, now and forever, like Yosemite and Yellowstone in the United States? What prevents us from doing so? Ice in our hearts? Blindness to the obvious?

A certain lack of boldness, I think.

It is time to turn on the lights. What is reasonable and what is not is all a matter of perspective. With the lights on, we can see that there are a lot of places on Earth worth saving.

One way I turned on the lights was to run full-page newspaper ads.

Way back in January 1969, in a page-and-a-half Sierra Club ad in the *New York Times*, we suggested that the whole Earth should be treated as a conservation district in the universe. The moon, Mars, and Saturn might be nice places to visit, but you wouldn't want to live there (Jupiter, these days, seems especially troubled). We also proposed the idea of treating the planet as a sort of Earth National Park. Our ad raised some eyebrows, paid for itself, and helped get me fired in 1969.

It also helped build support for the World Heritage system, which I consider the most important step in conservation since the national park idea emerged in 1864. The World Heritage idea was initiated a century later, in the 1960s, by Judge Russell Train, then president of the Conservation Foundation.

I watched his idea take place, supported by that January ad and by books from the Sierra Club and Friends of the Earth. In 1972 it was ratified by the United Nations. Since then, more than one hundred nations have approved more than four hundred areas of outstanding natural or cultural importance. Most of these places—such as Yosemite or Redwood National parks, the Grand Canyon, or the Parthenon—already had some kind of protection.

A group of us working with Russ Train came up with one hundred unprotected and endangered areas that to this day remain on a waiting list. The nations containing them have not yet seen fit to nominate them. World Heritage is a bold concept, one not yet completed.

THE GALÁPAGOS ISLANDS, of Ecuador, are in the World Heritage, thanks to many organizations and individuals, including Loren Eiseley, Russ Train, ecologist John Milton, and Eliot Porter, the photographer whose two great exhibit-format books on the islands, edited by Kenneth Brower, helped save Galápagos wildlife from eradication by colonialization. The islands were a big revelation for everybody, starting with Charles Darwin, who could be said to be the founder of modern ecology. Journeying to the Galápagos on the HMS *Beagle,* Darwin discovered that all life on the planet, from people to plankton, was part of a complex blanket spread over the globe. There can be no pulling of one thread in that blanket, without nubbing the weave, or worse, unraveling the fabric.

So I was glad to visit the Galápagos, at long last, once I finally got there on my way to the Earth Summit in Rio de Janeiro in 1992.

Our eldest son, Kenneth, visited the Galápagos twenty-five years before I did, and stayed three months. Among the many people he interviewed was Miguel Castro, the conservation officer of Darwin Station. Miguel's description of how tortoises die (an old tortoise may be 200) was interpreted by Ken in the Sierra Club volumes *Galápagos: The Flow of Wildness*: Once he gets big, a tortoise has no enemies, and if he avoids falling over a cliff or into a lava pit too steep for escape, he dies only of old age. One day he gets too weak to move, and stops. He stays in that spot for months, sometimes, his long-practiced power of enduring, his racial skill at it, serving him long after his power to move and get

53

food has failed. Watching leaves fall, probably, and the seasons change. . . . The tortoise living only in his head and eyes . . . a spark still somewhere inside, above the plastron and below the dome.

SIBERIA LIES FAR across the Pacific from the islands of the Galápagos, but the forests of Siberia circumscribe another of the jewels of the earth: Lake Baikal. Lake Baikal is the oldest, deepest lake on the planet. It holds one-fifth the world's liquid fresh water. Another fifth is held by our own Great Lakes, and another fifth by the waters of the Amazon. Baikal used to be three miles deep, but that was 25 million years ago. Sedimentation has built up on the bottom two miles. In short, it is still a deep lake.

In California and Nevada, our biggest lake is Tahoe. Tahoe would fit in a blustery cove of Baikal. Were it to be plopped down in our part of the world, Baikal would run from San Francisco to Tijuana—the length of California's Central Valley.

Lake Baikal, now a World Heritage site, is home to some 1,800 species that do not exist elsewhere. It is a treasure house of living treasures. Baikal holds the world's only landlocked freshwater seals, the nerpa, which are still hunted to get fur for hats. Of course, we (and the old Russians) hunted otters off North California long ago, and harp seals in northern Canada not so long ago, but today we know that this is a dumb idea.

Beauty has become as big an industry as lumbering, even mining, and certainly fur trading. Tourism has been estimated to be a trillion-dollar business on this planet, and eco-toursim is its cutting edge (although I would like to see the tour organizers remember to share the revenue fairly with the countries being toured). The Russians may miss the windfall if the nerpa are kept too nervous to be a tourist attraction. Killing exotic freshwater seals for fur has the same effect on tourism as machine-gunning elephants in Kenya for the ivory, or selling a lion hide for $1,000, while that lion, kept alive, could produce $500,000 in tourist revenue.

If cattle ranches in Australia are being turned into bird-watching sanctuaries, I hope the Russians will realize that one live nerpa willing to show off is worth a hundred that have been butchered.

ECOLOGICAL PRESERVES are not easy to create. Indigenous peoples are not eager to leave home just to please tourists (nor should they be forced to). It is generally a long, cool day before the individual country will nominate such a preserve. They have the same problem with developers we have. Developers have their own ideas about what to do with a resource such as Lake Baikal, the Grand Canyon, Mineral King, Mount Everest, or Hilton Head. They want to use it up. We just want it to last.

But why limit our thinking?

I'm now looking for help in turning on more lights in behalf of ecosphere reserves—the ecosphere being that part of the Earth that is life giving. We in the United States, brief tenants that we are, have an obligation to set a global example in truly wise use of land. We can respect the freedom of unnumbered future tenants. I like the goal of George Dyson, a bright young designer of seagoing canoes: "to find freedom without taking it from someone else." How many of the freedoms that we enjoy have been taken from other cultures?

To begin with, we can expand the Biosphere Reserve concept initiated by the U.N.'s "Man in the Biosphere Program." We can establish in the United States a National Ecoreserve System (NES). We now have reserves but no system. It took us fifty-two years from the first national park (Yosemite) to establish the National Park System in 1916, giving parks the protective clout they needed.

We can give our present biosphere reserves some recognition and clout by putting them in the NES. Add inadequately protected lands, federal, state, local, and private. Devise incentives to encourage private owners to help out. Establish performance standards—criteria for managing the land—to protect its biodiversity and provide some public access. Great Britain does this with its national parks, some privately owned. Wonderful signs guard the areas: "Please close the gate behind you" and "Be tidy." There's even one that says: "It is forbidden to cast stones at this notice. By order of the Surrey County Council."

To help this happen, change the name and mission of the Bureau of Land Management to the National Land Service (NLS). Give it a role in protecting *all* U.S. land, not just public land. Put the NES in the NLS. Easy to say. Hard to do. Essential to restoration and the future.

How about the rest of the world? How to get those areas on the waiting list of the World Heritage finally protected? How to go beyond World Heritage to protect areas of the Earth currently endangered, such as the forests of Siberia or the Amazon?

One way, and a good way to pay for this goal, would be to establish a World Ecological Bank (WEB), which would be as devoted to conserving, preserving, and restoring the Earth's ecological capital as the present-day World Bank is to expending it. WEB is a great acronym because it reminds us of the "webness" of life.

Through the WEB, nations could nominate areas of outstanding natural or cultural significance that reside in *other* nations. But through the WEB they would pay for the privilege. This would make it fair (or more fair) to the countries holding the designated areas, because it would defray the costs, and compensate those countries for the loss of old-fashioned extractive uses—logging, mining, and the rest—until alternative economic uses were developed for the areas as reserves that transcend national boundaries (economic uses that did not trash them), or until the host countries had the money to designate these areas as national parks.

By this process, interested WEB nations could nominate a substantial part of Tibet, for instance, as an international Peace Park. This is what the Dalai Lama has suggested. Until the Free Tibet effort succeeds, China could be paid to stop draining Tibet's natural capital.

Taiwan might be a nation willing to help pay to see Tibet's natural capital and great beauty spared, and we in the United States, Great Britain, or Germany might help pay Taiwan to change its appetite for tiger parts. Everybody should be willing to pay for the tiger nations, such as India, to protect their tigers.

In a sense, this is a global form of reverse colonialism. Parts of Canada and Southeast Asia could use some of the same help. Maybe even our own Pacific Northwest. Russia, certainly, could be paid to prohibit the clearcutting of Siberia's forests.

It is easy to be an alarmist if you comprehend what the vultures hovering over the pieces of the old Soviet Union are up to. They are trying to take everything they can get, chumming the Russians with hard cash. Actually, they are giving vultures a bad name. The oil companies want the oil. There's lots, and I'm not against our using oil, but I am against the rate at which we are exhausting it, be that in Alaska or Russia. The forest companies, such as Japan's Mitsubishi, are eyeing Siberia as if it were the new Amazon. To them it is. It should be to us, too, for different reasons.

The rain forests of Brazil, and forests of the rest of the Earth, are the lungs of the planet, putting out oxygen and locking up carbon. A quarter of the world's remaining forests are in Siberia. Those of us who are hooked on oxygen should be willing to pay Siberia to keep exporting oxygen instead of liquidating its forests.

I wish I were twenty years younger to work on this one.

I'd like to see if WEB could find a way to subsidize the maintenance of those magnificent Siberian forests. Ecologically sound selective cutting would help their economy without destroying yet another place most of us have not yet seen. (I can't forget Glen Canyon.) Nature, in trying to provide a surplus of everything, has let our numbers and also our appetites overdraw from that surplus. Without that overdraft, the trees in Siberia would be all right.

Another way to pay for "webness" would be to have every foundation in the world invest 10 percent of its equity in a revolving fund that would provide major financial backing to the new World Ecological Bank. This would be taking global the national example of the Nature Conservancy. It would allow foundations to make history.

The political power of foundation board members would strengthen the ability of respective governments to acquire and protect outstanding ecoreserves. The foundation investment could be recovered and reused. It could even be used to buy out exploiters. Let generous individuals—and governments—add to this World Ecological Fund of the World Ecological Bank.

I think a man like Russ Train, whom I consider the most outstanding Republican conservationist, should be put in charge of this Big Idea.

What we need in these perilous times is a consummate negotiator between the Earth and its human predators.

Let us now resolve to give the Earth the care we give—and this may surprise you—Yosemite. I've been going there for eighty-one years, and during that time the number of annual visitors grew from 37,000 to 4 million. Despite all those people, it looks better now that it did in 1918 or in the mid-thirties, when I worked there. I know of no other famous place that has pleased so many people and suffered so little impact.

I tell people who don't like the crowds in Yosemite Valley that I can take them in ten minutes to a place where they won't see anybody else all day. Unfortunately, the Park Service wants to build a parking lot there for 1,800 cars. Let's not let them! I'd rather see the old Yosemite Valley Railroad restored and electrified and the cars left at the train station. Cover the cost with sin taxes (and I'll pay my share gladly).

That's a better way to treat the world's first eco-preserve—if you don't count Eden.

CHAPTER 8

Forest Revolution

If today is a typical day on planet Earth, we will lose
116 square miles of rain forest . . .

—David W. Orr, environmental scientist

EVER SINCE the cedars of Lebanon started going down
to the sea in ships, we have failed to remember that photosynthesis makes it possible for creatures like us to breathe. The forest
and forest soil are the essential elements of the Earth's thin, dynamic, beautiful skin.

All over the world, we are running out of old growth trees—
our redwoods, Douglas firs and mahogany, pines and ipe, Sitka
spruce and teak, cedar and monkey puzzle. For a long time, paper
has been made from softwoods, such as fir and pine, but recent
technological advances allow giant timber corporations to pulp
hardwoods as well. The chain saws are being turned on mature
oaks in Mexico's Sierra Madre, soft maples in New England,
alders, poplars, and aspens, as well as countless tropical trees that
were once well off limits. Even cottonwoods, the gnarly giants

of rivers and riparian zones in the American West, are being ripped for cheap coffins. No tree is safe. The information society demands more, not less, paper for printers, copiers, and fax machines. Developing countries are converting their tropical hardwoods into textbooks. Democracy means more newsprint, and higher literacy calls for more books.

Simply put, what's left of the world's old growth forests is being savaged for two overweening purposes: building materials and paper pulp. A quarter of the trees cut down on the planet each year go to timber for two-by-fours, beams, plywood floor-ing, and the rest; while another eighth are killed to provide paper. There is also a horrendous desire for packaging materials, and in developing countries, a tremendous current demand for cooking fuel.

Everybody knows this. But what most people don't know is that it no longer has to be or can be this way.

We are on the verge of a forest revolution. It is not necessary to make paper from trees. It is no longer necessary that so many houses and buildings be constructed from wood and forest prod-ucts, at least not in the way we have become accustomed to in the United States, Canada, Japan, and Scandinavia. It is no longer necessary to use so much wood for cooking and heating. How do we change the way things are, to the way they ought to be? I have some ideas.

LET'S TAKE the easy one first: cooking fuel. One-half of the world's trees cut every year are cut for cooking fuel. Charcoal is just a lighter energy-intensive form of fuel wood, and it takes twice the energy to burn wood down to charcoal.

The long-term solution—and we need to expedite this right away—is solar cookers. These are tailor-made for the bare-necessity fuel users of the world, and there are billions of them. They have to eat, and if it's starch they have to cook it.

For the time being, however, natural gas is probably the most practical alternative, especially in the huge urban areas of the world's South. Nigeria and Mexico, for example, are major producers of natural gas, or could be. Two-thirds of the world's natural gas production is still burned off, or flared, at the wellhead. With the price of oil flat these days, the oil industry should welcome the opportunity to make out on gas and save forests in the process.

NOW THAT WE'RE warmed up, let's tackle some other problems that are chewing up our forests: papermaking and building materials. The obvious solution is to substitute other things for wood in the making of paper and in the construction of houses and commercial structures.

First, some good news. One of the largest builders of private homes in the United States, the Del Webb Corporation, has begun to replace wooden two-by-fours—the bone and sinew of modern architecture—with steel stud framing. There are some minor problems. It can be tricky, for example, to hang wallboard and sheetrock from steel, but pneumatic staplers have been invented that can puncture metal as well as wood. In the early 1990s Del

Webb and the United Steelworkers built about 100,000 new homes using steel instead of wood. The steel industry likes this development. Larger boards and beams are being fashioned from laminated wood, or engineered wood, as it is called, which is put together from smaller pieces using new glues, new processes—but beware of carcinogenic glues. This allows us to do something with all the pieces that would go to waste after the large boards have been cut.

The timber industry is also becoming more efficient. Technology has made it possible to take a look inside a tree, and then direct the cut with a computer, in order to eliminate waste and maximize the number of usable beams and two-by-fours. In the past, 40 percent or more of a felled log was considered unsuitable for lumber.

Some uses for lumber are even more wasteful. About 11,000 acres of Ohio forest are cut each year to make pallets, the wooden skids used everywhere—and tossed—in modern trucking and warehousing. Pallets can be made just as easily from plastic, and are beginning to be. In Europe pallets are recycled, like beverage bottles, and come with a returnable deposit.

Recycling wood is an idea for the coming decade, as Peter Warshall points out. Scrap wood clogs our landfills, but most of it can be recovered. Old pallets can be pulped. Houses can be dismantled by hand instead of by bulldozer. It's a labor-intensive process that could reduce homelessness. The wood can be reused instead of buried in landfill. Reuse will keep the wood's carbon locked up. This is not pie in the sky. It will be a whole new industry, much like the recycling of aluminum cans and glass bottles.

Already, especially in California, builders separate scrap wood when they are building and demolishing houses. Soon, landfill operators will be paying for that old lumber instead of charging to accept it—especially old barn siding that has been beautifully weathered.

Here's a challenge for the timber giant Weyerhaeuser, among others: For every 100 pounds of recyclable paper an environmentally concerned family turns in, will you guarantee to preserve as much primeval forest? For every 1,000 board feet of demolition lumber a green carpenter or construction company loads into your bins, will you agree to turn over as much ancient forest as it takes to make that amount of paper, or lumber, to, say, the Nature Conservancy? With the help of Justice Douglas, I got the Nature Conservancy its first $6 million line of credit. I like them.

What we need to do is to tie conservation directly to the preservation of old growth—a term subject to too many unhelpful interpretations. I prefer "primeval" or "ancient forest." I'm old growth myself, and that's not nearly old enough—or diverse enough. Biodiversity, varying beautifully from region to region, is what forests are all about.

My plan could have regional charm, in the United States, Europe, or anywhere. Caring people everywhere would know what biodiversity they were saving in their own bioregion. I believe this challenge would work, and we should try it.

Some of us—especially Americans, Canadians, Scandinavians, and the Japanese—are wood-lovers. This is not necessarily the case in hot, humid countries like the Philippines and Brazil, where the houses of wealthy people are often made of stone and cement, since wooden houses are subject to termites and other insects. In many tropical countries, it is the poor people who use cheap wood. We must encourage them to build from reinforced stone and adobe. Beautiful beams, redwood, teak, and mahogany, are still the high-end components of the gourmet housing industry. Here, perhaps, a cultural change is in order.

This wood is beautiful, but so is a polar bear rug or a sealskin hat. Many thoughtful consumers would not decorate their hearths with newly killed bear skin or wear real leopard. In the coming years, they may ask themselves if using giant redwood and mahogany is really such a good idea. They may decide, also, not to order from a mesquite grill, as they learn that old growth mesquite in Mexico and the American Southwest is being extinguished for mere human fashion, like beaver, like nerpa, like tiger.

I put redwood siding on our own house in 1946. I love it, but I would not use redwood again.

THE WORDS you are reading right now have not been printed on paper pulped from any tree. I write upon flowers, as it were. The paper in *Let the Mountains Talk* has been manufactured from kenaf, which is a twelve-foot cousin of cotton and okra, a variety of flowering hibiscus, *Hibiscus cannabinus*. Kenaf is a tough, fibrous annual, far richer in cellulose—which is what paper is made from—than is wood. Kenaf, and perhaps a couple of other timber—pulp substitutes, represents the next wave in saving the forests of the world.

The story of kenaf is interesting. In 1916 the United States government predicted the country could run out of trees by the end of the century. It was a prescient bit of forgotten science, that study. At the beginning of World War II, the U.S. Navy also did some hard thinking. Rope, once used rather a lot by sailors, was made from jute and hemp. It came mostly from the Philippines, which our then-opponents, the Japanese, controlled. The U.S. Department of Agriculture was asked to come up with some substitutes. They did a couple of studies, involving hundreds of plants. By process of elimination—what could be easily farmed? what made the best rope or paper?—kenaf, with hemp, came to the top of the list. And because of its longer fiber, kenaf may be recycled more easily than paper from wood pulp.

Some other people were not so hot on the idea. Dupont naturally preferred nylon for making rope, since they had invented it. They lobbied hard. (When you've been around awhile, you notice certain similarities. Dupont makes its money from nylon, from chemicals, not from farm products like kenaf. The automobile and tire companies make their profits from cars, and the oil companies from gas and oil. Standard Oil, General Motors, and Firestone lobbied successfully to rip out the municipal train tracks in Los Angeles and in some other American cities. No money was to be had from rail transportation, at least for them.) At any rate, Dupont won the rope wars. It did not hurt the argument that hemp was smoked by jazz musicians and African-Americans.

Kenaf did not carry hemp's psychoactive baggage, but after the war, further substitutes were no longer needed. There was nylon for rope. For paper, there were the glorious coastal temperate rain forests of Northern California, through Oregon, Washington, British Columbia, and right on to the Tongass forest in Alaska.

In the 1970s, when newsprint prices spiked a bit, those old kenaf studies were pulled off the shelf. The U.S. government paid to test some Illinois-grown kenaf between the rollers of the *Peoria Times*. It worked, but then newsprint prices dropped. There was still cheap pulp to be had from trees, and kenaf was again forgotten.

In the 1980s the big paper companies continued to marry the big lumber companies, and with so much go-go junk bond money around, they built very large mills, like nothing seen before on Earth. One of these supermills processes 400,000 tons of pulp a year. In the 1960s there were only one or two of these monsters. Now there are some fifty. In the 1960s there were more than 100 so-called mini-mills. Now there are only about thirty.

Is this good for anybody? Is it good for the Earth? Profits are now pitiful in the paper industry. Americans are out of work in the paper industry. The behemoths have severe overcapacity, and they are sucking up the forests of the planet to feed the maw. Anything is grist for the mill, and the scientists, instead of thinking up substitutes, are designing shredders and chemicals that can pulp any tree still living.

It is instructive to know that those countries, like China, which killed their trees and settled their wilderness long ago, no longer use trees for paper. They cannot. They have been forced to find substitutes, from rice to kenaf. I like to read. I like forests on the sides of my mountains. There is still a choice, for many countries.

Right now it costs more to make paper from kenaf than from cheap, heavily subsidized wood pulp. This is essentially a problem of start-up and of scale. More kenaf needs to be grown, and initially given a fraction of the subsidy wood gets. Smaller mills need to be built near kenaf farmlands. This will happen when the market is expanded. There was no market for recycled paper—what a strange idea—when I returned from World War II. Now thousands of companies do business on recycled paper. Recycled paper makes money, and it saves trees. In fact, if we could expand our use to about 40 percent, we would save an enormous amount of primeval forest.

By the way, it is important to realize that much of what passes for "recycled" is often no more than a byproduct of paper-making—the punched holes in notebooks, for instance, or envelope trimmings. True recycled paper is paper that has been used, recovered, repulped, and made into usable paper once more.

To create the market for tree substitutes, I would like to see the San Francisco and New York phone books printed on kenaf. How could that come about? Let's be bold. A lot of environmentalists live in those cities. Over 300,000 members of Greenpeace, alone, live in California, and there are some 1.7 million in the United States. There are 12 to 15 million dues-paying members of environmental organizations in the United States. That is a lot of requests for tree-free phone books, or, for that matter, bond stationery and book-quality printing paper. At the moment, kenaf is a high-end product. Stationery, cards, and books printed on kenaf already make good sense.

The federal government recently mandated that a certain percentage of its paper be printed on recycled wood fiber. Its departments should start using tree substitutes, like kenaf, in the same way, and also cotton and corn husks. The Italians and the Japanese are already doing it. The Germans are now the leaders in the multibillion dollar pollution-control industry. Must so much of American industry continually primp and posture as Detroit did thirty years ago, when its automakers scoffed at the visions of Volkswagen and Toyota?

Why does this happen? Because the timber and paper companies in this country (and the world) are far more heavily subsidized by their governments than the public suspects. They comprise a very powerful planetary country club. Taxpayers and consumers everywhere are being bled by the lumber barons of Japan, Canada, New York, and Houston because true costing, not to mention the cost to the Earth, is not invoked by industry economists. No wonder economist and futurist Hazel Henderson calls economics a form of brain damage.

It is a hidden subsidy to big timber for the taxpayer to pay the Forest Service for building roads into the best virgin forests. It is a hidden subsidy that these companies can come onto public land, clearcut the forests, and not even have to plant more. Or, if they plant more, to brag about the number of trees but forget to mention they are replacing an insignificant fraction of the volume they have removed. It will then be necessary for taxpayers, for generations to come, to cover the cost of replacing the excellence of, say, a 500-year-old tree and its surroundings. This is an enormous subsidy. When you add the cost to you of all these subsidies, you are probably paying far more—on April 15th of every year—for a book printed on wood pulp than for one printed on unsubsidized kenaf.

Will timber people once again, as they did under the Weeks Act in 1911, sell their derelict land at a profit to the government, which must pay (and charge taxpayers for) the restoration bill? Clearcutting and quick lumbering cause erosion. Erosion removes soil. Soil is what grows trees. That's a loss to future farmers. It is also a loss to pharmaceutical companies. So many drugs, from digitalis to quinine to yew-based cancer amelioratives, have been synthesized from forest plants, from primeval stands that are disappearing fast, as fast as one football field a second, in the tropical rain forests.

Politics can both cause the damage and require the cure. Why should the timber industry be allowed to kill the fishing industries of the United States, Canada, Mexico, Indonesia, the Philippines, and any other *terra firma* they chance to touch? Along with dams, the reason we don't have many salmon on the West Coast is largely because streams have been silted by clearcuts, which export soil and muddy the spawning beds.

At the moment, the governments of the world, certainly ours, value a tree only after it is cut down. But a tree has other responsibilities. Ask a bald eagle what the worth of a tree is. Ask a grizzly, who cannot prosper near roads cut into the forest. Ask the soil. Unless soil happens to be in a traveling mood, it values tree roots very highly. Especially after heavy rain.

And all over the Earth, even in our man-made deserts, a hard rain is beginning to fall.

Some of this rain is laced with acid from our factories. Using substitutes for lumber and for timber-pulp paper saves forests. Recycling saves forests. But in the northeastern United States, in eastern Canada, in Europe, acid rain is killing the trees before environmentalists and timber companies have a chance even to do battle over the end product. If we had less acid rain, we would have more forests.

There is a terrible word, in Germany, for what is going on. It is *waldsterben*: "forest death."

The Germans have gone as far as any of us in their attitude toward protecting forests. In Germany it is seen as a privilege to have trees on your property. In America, where some 73 percent of the forests are on private, not federal, lands you can do pretty much what you want with your trees. Not so in Germany. Germany issues tree licenses, much like driver's licenses. This would be pretty hard to swallow for many Americans, those that own trees, at least until they face their own death. Then the German system has its advantages. In America valuable trees are counted as assets. When an owner dies, the heirs must pay inheritance taxes on their value. This hurts, especially in the American South. To soften taxes in the United States, owners of beautiful forests cut them when they feel a certain chill. Or their children cut them soon after the funeral. This is stupid. It hurts the Earth.

Germany has tax incentives to maintain private forests, and we should have them, too.

If, in America, mortgage rates go up, housing starts go down. The price for timber falls. Suddenly, substitutes make less sense, outside the committed. When the dollar drops, that's worse. Then American timber is sold to Japan for a song. The Japanese are smarter than we are. They bury our old growth under water. They take the best logs from the Pacific Northwest, worth millions, and save them in the cold, preserving brine of their seas. To them, wood is gold. The price can only go up.

WE ARE ENTERING a twenty-year period that can either spell the end of beautiful trees as we know them, or that can save them. Here I want to stop and make some distinctions. What is really at stake right now is the primeval forest Longfellow admired in *Evangeline*. These are, usually, the closed canopy forests, perhaps the cathedral redwoods, where some of the trees tower 100 meters into the sky, or the Sitka spruce groves of British Columbia, or what is still virgin in the Amazon. What is no longer at stake are the gang-raped tropical rain forests of Papua New Guinea, Indonesia, and Malaysia. There will never be places like this on Earth again. We can save what's left. It is like saving the Grand Canyon. It must be done if enough of the pages of the poem that is the Earth are to remain whole.

Since 1600 the United States has lost 95 percent of its ancient forests. This does not mean that we don't have tremendous forests. The difference has been made up by secondary growth. In fact, in many states we are putting back in numbers as much as we are taking off. But in volume or in quality, we aren't even coming close. It is not the original good stuff, and of course it cannot be. Primeval forests represent the treasure troves of biodiversity and time. That is what makes them irreplaceable. You will never see again what we cut now; you will see nothing like it or the non-human community it nurtures.

IT IS NOT too late to practice sustainable eco-forestry. The mammoth monoculture tree plantations of Chile, New Zealand, and elsewhere are on the wrong track. This is crop farming, with Monterey pine as the soybean. But the vulnerability of monoculture has escaped the forestry schools, industry, and the Forest Service throughout this century. We need to use the product conservatively and grow forest diversity—not single-species plantations on the assumption that the Second Coming will spare us from tomorrow. We can reform. Public interest and private forestry can make sense, and need to.

There have been good timber companies and I have known good timber executives, such as Ike Livermore, a friend of mine and of wilderness for sixty years. I often disagreed with Ike, but never with rancor. When he was secretary of the Pacific Lumber Company, Ike liked to hear redwoods fall. But he didn't want too many redwoods to fall too soon, the way the takeover artists from Maxxam do. They acquired Ike's company in a hostile takeover in 1986, and are drastically overcutting to pay off their junk bonds and move on. Ike didn't advocate a thousand-year cutting cycle, which I think would be about right for redwoods, but his Pacific Lumber Company came closer to it than any other outfit in the board-foot crowd. And if you were a logger for Pacific Lumber, before it was chainsawed by Maxxam, you got about the highest wages in the industry, and even an $8,000 college scholarship for your kid.

I remember a conversation I once had with Pete Seeger, the great folksinger and champion of cleaning up the Hudson River. He said, "If you don't walk along with someone as far as possible, there can be no conversation." So walk with people you do not agree with, gathering their point of view. Put yourself in their shoes, prepared to learn and to persuade. If that doesn't work, it's time for full-page ads, time to marshal the troops, by the millions if you've got them. They are there, because everybody breathes and our very atmosphere is at risk. There is only one Earth.

The environmentalists of the world must not be so naive as to think they have won if they stop Maxxam, Mitsubishi, the timber princes of Djarkata, or Burger King from killing ancient forest stands from British Columbia to Costa Rica to Montana to the Penang Peninsula. Rust never sleeps. There is a timber industry term called *coyoting*. If logging isn't profitable on one forest, trot over the ridge to the next. Douglas fir in Canada makes terrific pulp. Canada's environmentalists raise a hue and cry? Maybe Mexican tree-huggers are not yet so well organized. Pulp is pulp and old growth oak on the Sierra Madre squishes just as well.

We who would defend the Earth must look in the mirror. We are endangered. Time is running out. If a small child wields a kitchen knife, you do not try to wrestle it away. You offer a substitute—a toy, a cookie, anything. If we want a future by design, not default, it's time for a rebirth of creativity. History tells us all too clearly what it costs to run out of forests. Man has created deserts with great skill in the past, and is speeding the process today.

By buying this book, printed on kenaf, you contribute toward the rescue of forests in Siberia, Canada, the United States, and everywhere else. Earth Island Institute paid a little more for this paper, but we all get paid back in the long run, by the taxes you and coming generations will not have to pay to subsidize the unnecessary pulping of forests.

You are helping build the demand that will encourage others to meet it. And there is further reward in your knowing that the unpulped trees can keep a lot of forest beautiful in perpetuity. That kind of perpetuity brought the forests from prehistory to you. Let it remain the essential element in what Wallace Stegner, one of the most creative of writers, called the Geography of Hope.

CHAPTER 9

More Monks

Trend is not destiny.
—René Dubos

ASKED HOW MANY people the Earth can sustain indefinitely, Harvard professor E. O. Wilson, certainly one of the world's great biologists, replied: "If they have the appetite for resources of Japan and the United States, 200 million." This was reported to me in Kyoto by Dr. David Suzuki, Canadian biologist and commentator. I'd never heard so low a figure, and finally got Professor Wilson on the telephone to check up. Had he said that? "No," he responded, "but it sounds reasonable."

He gave me some people to refer to further, including population researcher and author Anne Ehrlich. She gave me an estimate at the 1991 Land, Air, and Water Conference, in Eugene, Oregon: "With a little more industrial development in the Third World, 500 million."

SOLUTIONS

In other words, the Earth is now supporting (but not very well) ten times more people than it can handle over the long run. We are surviving by severely overdrawing life's account in the World Resource Bank. OK so far, as the man said after falling forty stories with only ten to go.

Somewhere I picked up a staggering statistic: In the past fifty years the United States has used up more resources than all the rest of the world in all previous history. I haven't checked that figure. I like it the way it is. If it isn't right yet, we seem determined to make it right. Wrong.

"Trend is not destiny," the late René Dubos wrote. I do not blindly oppose progress. I oppose blind progress. We had better not let the U.S. trend become the Earth's destiny. We don't need to.

I don't know about life after death, but I do believe in life after birth. And it is absolutely essential that we take steps to make that life after birth a better one. Here are some key steps to take. Try hard not to be offended by them:

First, improve the literacy of women and leave the number of children to be born up to them—the nurturers, not the passersby.

Second, improve nutrition and medical care and thus reduce the number of children thought necessary for survival of our species.

Third, improve all other forms of social security for the same reason. Remember James Reston's admonition when he was a *New York Times* editor: "We have no more right to tell a man how many children he may have than how many wives he may have."

78

I found myself unable to stop telling this admonition in time when addressing an audience in Utah, and escaped by pointing out that the number of children is a social problem, and the number of wives merely an organizational problem.

Perhaps someone should take the Pope to lunch and explain things to him. Perhaps the Dalai Lama should. He told a Berkeley audience on a sunny day in 1994: "The solution to the population problem is—more monks!"

CHAPTER 10

Hypercars

Ready or not, we're all about to embark on one of the
greatest adventures in industrial history.

—Amory Lovins

I WAS LISTENING to Amory Lovins last year. Amory
was saying: "The biggest change in industrial structure since
the microchip will be a revolution in what cars are, how they're
made, how they're sold, and even how they're driven. I call these
vehicles—*hypercars*."

When Amory talks, I am careful to listen. He is usually right
as rain—rain before we added acid. I also like a modest beginning:
"the biggest change in industrial structure since the microchip."
And I know that if hypercars come on-line soon, environmentalists, like everyone else, will have some retooling to do. Or it will
be a wilder century than we all might like to think.

Amory Lovins was once a don at Merton College, Oxford
University, and I think he was the youngest fellow to hold that

position in 400 years. He was shaking things up at Harvard when he was sixteen. He completed his undergraduate experience long before reaching the drinking age—which he has declined to exploit. I've never persuaded him to take a drink. Sometimes I think that one of my greatest achievements was persuading Amory Lovins to give up being a don. He was in physics then. Just soon enough, he invented the soft energy path.

After he returned to the United States, Amory wrote a paper for Bill Bundy at *Foreign Affairs* called "Energy Strategy: The Road Not Taken," which was the most popular article *Foreign Affairs* ever published.

Amory challenged everything. He said America had too much energy, that the hydro-nuclear-coal-electric grid was silly, often unnecessary, heavily subsidized by the taxpayers, danger-ous, and uneconomic, that the peaceful atom was a myth masking a bloated war machine, and why bother, anyhow? This shook some of us, but Amory had the figures to back himself up. He always does. Then he suggested some ways out of the jungle: solar and efficiency. Amory cofounded the Rocky Mountain Institute near Aspen. He designed its stone and wood building's energy systems so that even at 40 degrees below zero, it is 99 percent solar-heated.

Some people have scoffed at Amory, because, quiet as he is, he rocks their boat. But some people have changed their lives according to Amory's predictions; others have unscoffed all the way to the bank. So when Amory began to talk of hypercars, I was prepared to listen, and I hope you are, too. I turn this chapter over to the capable hands of Amory Lovins.

The Hypercar™ represents a leapfrog in the art of designing and building cars. The Hypercar artfully fuses together the best available technology for ultralight construction and hybrid-electric drive. I want to emphasize the synergy between these two technologies. People have made ultralight cars. They weigh two to three times less than normal cars, and they're about two or two-and-a-half times more efficient. People have also made hybrid-electric cars, but if you put hybrid drive in a heavy car, it only improves efficiency by about 30 percent to 50 percent. If you put ultralight and hybrid together in the same car, which is just starting to be done, then you're getting a factor of four to eight gain in efficiency. It's one of those "1 + 2 = 5" equations.

Hypercars will get 100 to 200 miles per gallon, and could possibly get even more. The Hypercar burns 100 or even 1,000 times cleaner than present cars. Fuel-cell versions will emit nothing but water. Hypercars will be sturdier, safer, sportier, more comfortable, beautiful, durable, and quiet—and just generally *nicer* than present cars. They may even cost less.

But they're profoundly different in many ways, and therefore, come up against cultural barriers within the automaking industry. Also, though Hypercars buy us time, they cannot solve the transportation problem, and, indeed, may make it worse, by making driving even cheaper and more attractive than it is now.

How is this all possible? Let me spend a minute on the physics of cars. After decades of devoted incremental effort, only about 15 to 20 percent of fuel energy manages to reach the wheels. (Ninety-five percent of the vehicle's motion moves the car, so only 1 percent of the fuel energy moves the driver.) Why is that? Cars are conventionally made of steel. Steel is heavy. It takes a lot of force to accelerate something heavy, so conventional car engines are so oversized that their average efficiency is cut in half. The energy that finally does reach the wheels is dissipated in three equal shares in city driving: heating the air that the car pushes aside, heating the tires and road, and heating the brakes when you stop. In other words, one-third of the delivered wheel-power in a conventional car goes to heat the air, one-third to heat the tires and road, and one-third to heat the brakes.

The ultralight strategy is to make the car three times lighter (yet safer, too); make it nearly three times more slippery so that it can cut through the air more easily; and reduce the tire and road heating by a factor of 3 to 5. Finally, the electric drive motors can convert braking energy back into reusable electricity.

Basically, the Hypercar is designed like an airplane

rather than a tank. The outside can be smaller. The inside is bigger. I call it state-of-the-shelf technology. The shell of the car is made of advanced composites, chiefly carbon fibers—very light, fairly expensive per pound, but so cheap to manufacture that the total cost is similar. When you put the family inside with the suitcases and the dog, the payload could weigh more than the car.

The hybrid-electric drive part of the Hypercar means that the wheels are driven mostly or wholly by electricity. The Hypercar would not be battery driven because fuel has 100 times as much energy per pound as batteries. Rather, the Hypercar would use a tiny engine, gas turbine, or (best of all) hydrogen fuel cell, to make electricity onboard from fuel, as needed.

Let me make this a little more real. A plain old ultralight prototype has already been built. It is called the "GM Ultralite." Two copies were built in 1991 by fifty people in 100 days at General Motors at a cost of about 4 to 6 million dollars, which was equivalent to about eight hours' worth of the company's North American losses at that time. Inside, it's as big as a Corsica. Outside, it's as small as a Miata. It weighs 1,400 pounds, including four airbags. The shell is light carbon fiber (though it could be a lot lighter). The engine is a tiny little thing, smaller than a Honda Civic engine, and yet it matches the acceleration of a 12-cylinder BMW—zero to sixty in 7.8

seconds—because it's so light. Top speed is 135 miles per hour. You can go directly to jail on any highway on Earth. If the ultralite had a hybrid drive, it could get about 110 to 200 miles per gallon, rather than 62.

Amory believes Detroit is halfway there but may not make it up the hill. Too many cultural barriers.

Imagine that the Big Three typewriter makers—like the Big Three car makers—were about one-seventh of the U.S. Gross National Product, directly and indirectly. You remember typewriters, don't you? Over the decades, typewriter makers have gone from manual to electric, and let's say they're now working on the subtle incremental refinements for the forthcoming Selectric 17. These are good typewriters, the Selectric 17s. The Big Three probably sell 12 million of them a year. There's only one little problem coming over the horizon. Namely, the competition is working on wireless subnotebook computers.

This is where the steel-car industry is today. It is exquisitely sophisticated and good at what is does. It is the highest expression of the Iron Age. And it is fundamentally obsolete.

The big automakers start with two disadvantages, as energy expert Lee Schipper said: they're big and they're automakers. It's really tough to change a die-making, steel-stamping culture into a molded-synthetics, electronics, and software culture. What I'm discussing is really much more like a computer with wheels than it is like a car with chips. Maybe the companies that will do it best will not be automakers at all, but the Hewlett-Packards of the world, the systems integrators who learn fast.

Not many people in Detroit understand something we should have learned from the wreckage of IBM's mainframe computer business: that you have to kill your own products with better new products before someone else does. As they say at 3M, "We'd rather eat our own lunch, thank you."

If you don't take risks, Amory believes, you may be put out of business by the first corporation that leapfrogs, thereby turning Detroit's incremental improvements strategy into a bet-your-company strategy. "That competitor may not be Honda," he adds. "It may be a bunch of smart, hungry aerospace engineers in a garage in Southern California, or Singapore, or Switzerland—people you've never heard of, who are off your radar, the next Apple."

Now, at this point, I should say I only acquired my first Apple PowerBook at age eighty-two. We recently had two cars, my wife and I—a 1983 Toyota, and a 1968 Volvo with 267,000 miles on it. There are only 160,000 on the Toyota, and the Volvo just went to the glue factory. I am ready for a Hypercar. But is the world?

In some respects, yes. We're paying $50 billion a year for oil imports in this country alone. Factor in the cost of keeping the peacetime army in trim, so that it is always ready to intervene in the Persian Gulf and protect the sludge at the wellhead, and the cost of oil becomes very expensive indeed. Amory points out that about three-fifths of the air pollution emitted by cars in this country puffs and spurts from only one-fifth of our car fleet. If we made the switch to Hypercars, there would be a lot less pollution and we would all save a lot of fuel dollars. Since Amory's Hypercars are more reliable and simpler to fix, the mechanic can just come out to your house. Since they can be manufactured quickly, requiring no years of expensive retooling, you'll probably be able to order one by phone. They'll build it when they receive your check, and send it out—like L. L. Bean, only on a bigger truck. There is no need for a Hypercar sales force. Over half the people involved in making and selling today's cars can be chalked up to the old way of showrooming automobiles.

This little revolution is going to put a few people out of work, especially if Detroit wakes up as slowly as it did to my buying cars from Volkswagen, Toyota, and Volvo, and giving up on Ford, Mercury, Pontiac, Buick, and Chevrolet. Amory informs me that the United States is ahead in all the relevant technology and will gain more jobs than it loses. However, as far as "the national interest" is concerned, the future could swing either way. "There are," says Amory, raising eyebrows, "unique opportunities, let us say, for rapid market entry"—then he smiles—"and rapid market exit" on the part of the steel-car companies.

"Ready or not," concludes my friend Amory Lovins, "we're all about to embark on one of the greatest adventures in industrial history."

Are environmentalists ready? The implications for them are as strong as they are for car manufacturers. We won't be in danger of running out of oil anymore, or at least for a much longer time, and our air stands a chance of becoming much cleaner. But we will run out of roads and pavement, because so many more people in so many more countries will be able to afford hypercars. And what will this mean for rapid transit outside urban areas? The beautiful curse of the automobile will not leave us. Environmentalists were right about cars in the first place. What we will need in the era of the hypercar, then more than ever, is less automobility through better land-use policies. Those cities with boundaries that I mentioned earlier, which put work closer to home and leave the Big Outside restored and wild, must become bare necessity, if we are all not to be flattened by the future. Let the car be a pet, not a workhorse.

PART III

Restoration

CHAPTER 11

A World Restored

Latent in the restoration movement, we can imagine a
potential not simply to change the direction of Western
culture but to alter its foundation.

—Barry Lopez

BROKEN EGGS must remain broken, but broken hearts
may be mended with love. Extinct species are gone, but
endangered plants and animals may be brought back from the
brink. Exhausted fields can renew themselves. Grass can annihi-
late pavement. So long as life lasts, dashed hopes stand a chance.
We need only get over that current feeling that says, "Where
there is life there must be hopelessness." We must ever answer
the question "But what can I do?" with the realization that
restoring the Earth, making things better, renews and heals us at
the same time.

Restoration is a deceptively complex concept. It means re-
generation. Return the natural world to the way it was, as best
we can, before clearcutting, acid mining, inelegant development,

pollution and the industrial accidents of bygone eras harmed the Earth. Give nature a jump start, and stand back.

Restoration means putting the Earth's life-support systems back in working order: rivers, forests, wetlands, deserts, soil, and endangered species, too. Many dams on many rivers have been made unnecessary by new systems of energy generation and distribution. Let's take out those superfluous dams, beginning with Yosemite's Hetch Hechy, which never should have been dammed, and let's drain Glen Canyon. We need forests, not just tree plantations. Wetlands, as we are beginning to learn, purify our drinking water, acting like giant filters. Ducks like them, too. Deserts require reclamation, not inundation. And isn't it about time we stopped treating soil like dirt?

Human systems also need restoration. Let's rehabilitate the South Bronx, and all the other places like it across the Earth. To accomplish that, we must give the unemployed and the never-employed a stake in the wider restoration process. Let's also put environmental conscience into world trade and into our corporate thinking. It is time corporations moved from green public relations to green operations, so far as their environmental strategy is concerned. Restoration departments should be added to whatever Departments of the Interior are called the world around, and to the World Bank, while eco-spin—meaning that you carry on with your work, but you carry on with the best interests of the Earth as you do so—should be included in every thinking person's job description, from farmer to architect.

Of late, there has been an epidemic of cynicism, a general inability to understand how right Richard Barnet was when he said, "We march toward annihilation under the banner of Realism."

Whatever and whoever has brought humanity to the edge of the chasm probably just thought they were being practical. Practical people, as has been pointed out, are those who have made all their decisions, lost the ability to listen, and are determined to perpetuate the errors of their ancestors. They have all the foresight implicit in this advice: "When you reach the fork in the road, take it."

More people need to understand that milk does not come from a plastic container, or water from a valve, or gasoline from a throttle. The sources of human wealth have been provided for by nature on the only planet most of us are ever likely to reside upon comfortably. The Earth's ecological capital has been sorely overdrawn. We are running out of the things that fuel economic growth.

"If today is a typical day on the planet Earth," writes environmental scientist David W. Orr in *Earth in Mind*, "we will lose 116 square miles of rain forest, or about an acre a second. We will lose another 72 square miles to encroaching deserts, the results of human mismanagement and overpopulation. We will lose 40 to 250 species, and no one knows whether the number is 40 or 250. Today the human population will increase by 250,000. And today we will add 2,700 tons of chlorofluorocarbons and 15 million tons of carbon dioxide to the atmosphere. Tonight the Earth will be a little hotter, its waters more acidic, and the fabric of life more threadbare."

HARD-CORE statistics like Orr's are an essential wake-up call. I have a younger friend named Severn Cullis-Suzuki, who spoke at the plenary session of Earth Summit in Rio de Janeiro in June 1992, when she was twelve years old. This was the speech the future vice president, Al Gore, liked best of all, according to biologist David Suzuki, her father. I can think of nothing more important to restoration than the restoration of hope in children. I show the video of her wake-up call every time I get the chance:[1]

Hello, I'm Severn Suzuki. . . .

Coming up here today, I have no hidden agenda. I am fighting for my future. Losing my future is not like losing an election or a few points on the stock market. . . .

I am afraid to go out in the sun now because of the holes in the ozone. I am afraid to breathe the air because I don't know what chemicals are in it. I used to go fishing in Vancouver with my dad until just a few years ago we found the fish full of cancers. And now we hear about animals and plants becoming extinct every day—vanishing forever.

---

[1]The full text and story appears in a beautifully illustrated children's book, *Tell the World: A Young Environmentalist Speaks Out*, by Severn Cullis-Suzuki (Doubleday Canada Limited, 1993).

In my life, I have dreamed of seeing the great herds of wild animals, jungles and rainforests full of birds and butterflies, but now I wonder if they will even exist for my children to see. Did you have to worry about these little things when you were my age?

All this is happening before our eyes and yet we act as if we have all the time we want and all the solutions. I'm only a child and I don't have all the solutions, but I want you to realize, neither do you!

You don't know how to fix the holes in our ozone layer.

You don't know how to bring salmon back up a dead stream.

You don't know how to bring back an animal now extinct.

And you can't bring back the forests that once grew where there is now desert.

If you don't know how to fix it, please stop breaking it!

Here you may be delegates of your governments, businesspeople, organizers, reporters, or politicians. But really you are mothers and fathers, sisters and brothers, aunts and uncles. And each of you is somebody's child. . . .

Two days ago here in Brazil, we were shocked when we spent some time with some children living on the streets. . . .

I can't stop thinking that these children are my own age, and that it makes a tremendous difference where you are born. I could be one of those children living in the *favellas* of Rio. I could be a child starving in Somalia, a victim of war in the Middle East or a beggar in India.

I'm only a child yet I know if all the money spent on *war* was spent on ending poverty and finding environmental answers, what a wonderful place this Earth would be.

At school, even in kindergarten, you teach us to behave in the world. You teach us:

not to fight with others

to work things out

to respect others

to clean up our mess

not to hurt other creatures

to share, not to be greedy.

Then why do you go out and do the things you tell us not to do?

Parents should be able to comfort their children by saying, "Everything's going to be all right"; "We're doing the best we can" and "It's not the end of the world." But I don't think you can say that to us anymore. Are we even on your list of priorities?

My dad always says, "You are what you do, not what you say."

Well, what you do makes me cry at night.

You grown-ups say you love us. I challenge you, *please*, make your actions reflect your words.

Thank you for listening.

I BELIEVE some adults were listening in 1992. It was a year that the world seemed to examine itself, like a marble held in a child's hand, something we had not done since the first moon landing or the original Earth Day. In 1992 more than 2,000 concerned scientists spoke out. Perhaps they had heard Severn. Among these scientists were 102 Nobel laureates:

> No more than one or a few decades remain before the chance to avert the threats we now confront will be lost and the prospects for humanity immeasurably diminished. A new ethic is required, a new attitude toward discharging our responsibility for caring for ourselves and for the earth. This ethic must motivate a great movement, convincing reluctant leaders and reluctant peoples themselves to effect needed change.

It is time to visualize that proper new ethic. It is time to reweave life's fragile web. It is time, finally, to begin to restore what we and our "practical" ancestors have so carelessly destroyed.

By restoring the Earth, we have the opportunity to invest in ecological sanity, to reinvest in prosperity, to invest in an understanding of how nature works and what we have to do to let it work. It is healing time on Earth. Of course, we should not be so arrogant as to think that we've got all the answers, because we haven't. If we're not careful, we could make the old mistakes, such as bringing rabbits to Australia, the mongoose to Hawaii, or something perhaps even worse, like a chemical overdose to the human fetus on its fifty-sixth day, when its decision to be male or female can be confused.

As an economic engine, restoration will prove to be a boon to the economies of the world. It is a movement, already begun, that I believe will come to involve millions of people, young and old, in what I have called CPR for the Earth—Conservation, Preservation, and Restoration. I hope it will also engage the great religions, savvy armies, and powerful corporations both altruistic and shrewd. After all that, even governments might follow.

I started out as a boy bent over a spring. Then I climbed mountains. I became a conservationist. Then I saw what we all were doing, and I wanted to stop us from doing worse. Now I want to restore what once was, not for an old man's memories, but for a baby's smile.

CHAPTER 12

Making a Difference

The wilderness holds answer to more questions
Than we yet know how to ask.
    —Nancy Newhall

SOMETIMES IT SEEMS to me the restoration movement
started itself. Perhaps the Earth whispered Aldo Leopold's "goose
music" into the ears of isolated individuals, and they were moved
by the honking. Perhaps things had got so bad in some places that
certain men and women just wanted it put back the way it was, and
possessed the visionary moxie to do the putting, to see restoration
through. These individuals are like travelers lost in the wild, who
want to go back to the last recognizable landmark and look again
for the next. Restoration is not an effort to stop the clock, but
rather a chance to keep the clock running—in fact, our best
chance.

In the last two or three decades, people, like seeds, have
planted themselves in ravaged terrain and begun to do some

work—from Bermuda's Nonesuch Island to the despoiled Mattole River of Northern California, to the moonscape of Auroville in India, to the banks of the Nashua River in New Hampshire, to the urban war zones of the South Bronx, to the cement quarries of Kenya, to the polluted Neva River of the old Soviet Union and the "living dead" that Dan Janzen found in the scattered debris of the dry tropical forest of Costa Rica, as I'll explain in a minute. Without fanfare, these unlinked humans have begun to make a difference. They are fixing the soil, bringing back the salmon and the not-quite-extinct cahow, and helping the homeless to help themselves.

Some pretty big projects are being undertaken. Money is being raised and money is being spent, generating jobs and sustaining careers as well as regenerating the trashed Earth. Major new players, a new breed of engineering firm and a new type of green corporation, have begun to fly on the side of the angels. A new field of endeavor has been created, with hydrologists and botanists changing things for the good. There is now a restoration industry, and "systemic problems rather than symptoms are being addressed," as John Berger puts it. The return of the meandering Kissimmee, or what most people would call the saving of the Florida Everglades, is an example of what can happen when individual obsession steamrolls politicians, and everybody suddenly discovers that they are doing the right thing, by themselves and by the Earth, and at the same time.

I had heard about some of these efforts, small and big, when I was president of Friends of the Earth. But I first began to fathom the significance of what was happening—that our species was finally, spontaneously, and gloriously making a U-turn—after I read two remarkable books, *Restoring the Earth*, by John Berger, and *Helping Nature Heal*, edited by Richard Nilsen.

What follows are a few examples that I like to savor, of regenerating soil, islands, forests, and rivers.

Alan Lithman begins his account of "Revisiting Auroville" in *Helping Nature Heal*:

> We were dragging our bicycles across the barren fields avoiding the sharp stubble, all that was left by the migrant herds of cows and goats. A merciless sun beat down upon this wretched piece of earth, bleaching it bone white or a brittle terra-cotta. A once-living earth dying back into a moon. We reached the edge of a canyon whose fingers gouged through the landscape. My friend pointed across the ravine to the barren plateau beyond, where a few palmyra trees shimmered like phantoms in the heat waves. "There it is," he said, "Auroville." I looked and saw nothing but a vacant landscape that slid into the Bay of Bengal. How could I possibly live there? How could anyone?

This was how Tamil Nadu in southern India looked in 1969, denuded by generations of subsistence agriculturists. Twenty-five years later, more than two million indigenous trees have been planted. A soft lip of forest greens the sunsets. I was taken with a diagram of how cleverly those trees were planted. A square hole was dug into barren rock with a *mumpti*, what we might call a garden adz. The cube shape induced the roots to grow into the corners, so they would not circle around themselves. Trees planted on hillsides were dug with a groove in the mulched rim so that rainwater naturally flowed down to them, and was caught.

But I was struck as much by Lithman's philosophical understanding of what was going on as by his practical wisdom:

> We have all been colonialists on this planet. At Auroville, there was simply no buffer with which to fool ourselves. [They were down to laterite, rock without soil, a bad spot to be in, if you want to grow things.] It was clear what had to be done, and there was no one else to do it for us. We were humanity coming home to repay a terrestrial debt from the West to the East, a karma that we owed to the earth.

DAVID WINGATE began his Caribbean restoration project a long time ago, before even Auroville. As a schoolboy on Bermuda, he had an unusual interest in birds. His precocious enthusiasm caused him to be invited on a passionate expedition in the late 1940s to discover if there were any cahows still alive. The cahow is a Caribbean seabird, a type of petrel related to the albatross. Cahows were thought to have checked out in the 1600s when the Spanish and British decimated this part of the Caribbean by introducing pigs and logging the original cedar forests for shipbuilding.

Here is how Wingate describes their rediscovery: "I will never forget the elation on Dr. Murphy's face when he and Mowbray succeeded in noosing a bird out of its deep nesting crevice, held it up to the light, and exclaimed, 'By Gad, the cahow!'"

By Gad, the cahow! I laughed when I read that. But I wonder why no one laughs when the *New York Times* reports that there are now 360 billionaires in the world, 200 of them in the United States. Somewhere along the line we have misplaced our priorities. David Wingate is a saint, more so than St. Francis, who only allowed the squirrels to sit upon his lap. Wingate took a certain knowledge of biology and set about to rebuild the ecosystem of Nonsuch Island, planting 8,000 trees by himself, taking out the introduced rats with warfarin, nurturing old plant and animal species still around from precolonial times, hand-feeding the nestlings of the yellow-crowned night heron with chopped-up land crabs. He has created a living museum of what once was, and could be again.

Nonsuch Island. Such a beautiful name. There will be many more such places.

FOR SEVEN YEARS I have been unable to make a speech without talking about Daniel Janzen of the University of Pennsylvania, the ecological consultant to Foundaçion Neotropica, in San José, Costa Rica. The beginning of his article in *Science*, "Tropical Ecological and Biocultural Restoration," always scares me, though his solutions cheer me. This important paper begins:

> The increasingly vigorous efforts to protect some of the relatively intact portions of tropical nature come too late and too slow for well over half the tropics—especially the half best suited to agriculture and animal husbandry. Its relatively intact habitats are gone. Its remaining wildlands are hardly more than scattered biotic debris. The only feasible next step is conservation of biodiversity by using the living biotic debris and inocula from nearby intact areas to restore habitats. If this step is not taken quickly, natural and anthropogenic perturbations will extinguish most of the habitat remnants, small population fragments, and the living dead—the organisms that are living out their physiological life spans, but are no longer members of persistent populations.

Who has scattered this "biotic debris," in which Janzen includes the "living dead"? You and I and our time on Earth.

Janzen explains how restoration may be jump started, and how he has begun to accomplish this necessary miracle himself.

First, there must be "an adequate inoculum of plants and animals," and these must be "permitted to invade and grow":

> Choose an appropriate site, obtain it, and hire some of the former users as live-in managers. Sort through the habitat remnants to see which can recover. Stop the biotic and physical challenges to those remnants. The challenge is to turn the farmer's skills at biomanipulation to work for the conservation of biodiversity. . . .
>
> Human cultures evolved in mutualism and conflict with the natural world. . . . Tropical humans are experiencing nearly total loss of this integral part of their mental lives. It is as though they are losing their color vision and most of their hearing.

AS NANCY NEWHALL wrote in *This Is the American Earth*, the first of the Sierra Club's exhibit-format books, inspired by Ansel Adams: "The wilderness holds answers to more questions than we have yet learned how to ask."

At our peril do we pulp and shred those answers. If in all too many places all that is left are scattered biotic debris and the living dead, we had better begin to join them together once more, to restore them in order to restore our own minds as well.

Large ecosystems, once wild, may also undergo the process. It is instructive to consider the Everglades. To settlers in Florida, the Everglades were a useless wasteland that frustrated their efforts to raise cattle and sugarcane. Anything that could be done to remove the threat of flooding and transform the swampy prairie into pasture was deserving of unqualified support. The heart of the whole messy system was the Kissimmee River, a sluggish body of water that could not be easily controlled.

In the 1960s the Army Corps of Engineers straightened the kinks in the Kissimmee, shortening the river from 97 miles to 54. A canal was built down the middle, straight as a crow's flight and longer. The old meandering oxbows were left to bleach in the Florida sun, along with millions of animals and rare plants, among them wading birds, alligators, deer, and Florida panthers. Soon the purity of the water at the bottom end of the state, serving major cities, turned bad. It seems that the useless floodplain of the Everglades had served as one of those giant filtering fans, slowly cleansing the sheet of water as it flowed south, recharging the aquifer. The only thing gained was, in effect, enormous subsidies for sugar corporations and cattle growers—and a river flowing faster than it was designed to flow.

In the 1970s the losses to cities through degraded drinking water became politically obvious. Everglades that were drying up were also becoming far less attractive to tourists, and tourism had become an industry ten times bigger than sugar and cattle, a story being repeated across the world.

In the 1980s the Sierra Club, the Audubon Society, and a small army of volunteers joined with rising Florida politicians such as Bob Graham, who would become a U.S. Senator, to restore the Everglades. Steel weirs were built across the upper Kissimmee Canal, which slowed the flow and backed water into the old oxbows. Once again, the water was cleaned by natural processes, grasses, and settling. Herons, alligators, and panthers have begun their return.

Graham's goal is to have the Everglades look and function the way they did in 1900.

SOME FARSIGHTED people are thinking about restoring another large ecosystem, the "buffalo commons." Many counties on the Great Plains and in arid regions of eastern Montana and the Dakotas are not doing so well agriculturally. They rarely have done well, except in years of unusually high rains. Perhaps these places would work better the old way, with buffalo restored to the tall grass with which they coevolved. Coevolution requires a symbiotic relationship that I believe buffalo could handle and cows don't. Far from removing humans from these areas, a buffalo commons might provide new eco-tourist dollars for depressed small towns. Humans would cluster themselves outside the buffalo reserves, just as they do now within agricultural centers.

The bison would move among the restored areas, along wildlife corridors. Imagine: bison underpasses below the occasional human interstate. In Berkeley's Tilden Park, we have signs on the roadway that say "Newt Crossing" and have even closed a park road during the mating season to allow the newts to cross safely in the essential search of each for the other.

Should I tell Mr. Gingrich about this?

CHAPTER 13

The CPR Service

> We travel together, passengers on a little space ship,
> dependent upon its vulnerable reserves of air and soil, all
> committed for our safety to its security and peace, preserved
> from annihilation only by the care, the work and, I will say,
> the love we give our fragile craft.
>
> We cannot maintain it half fortunate, half miserable,
> half confident, half despairing, half slave to the ancient
> enemies of mankind and half free in a liberation of
> resources undreamed of until this day. No craft, no crew,
> can travel safely with such vast contradictions. On their
> resolution depends the survival of us all.
>
> —Adlai Stevenson, July 1965

FROM TIME immemorial our kind has fought wars.
But we cannot have peace on the Earth without making peace
with the Earth. I was a combat veteran of World War II, the war
Studs Terkel called "the last good war." I entered as a private,
retired as a major, and had a hand in teaching ten thousand
younger men to climb mountains. Before too long, other young
men would be shooting at them, and they needed to know how

to handle rough terrain as well as the enemy when the time came.

Just before the war's end, the Germans were retreating across the Po Valley. When you retreat, tactics require that you leave some soldiers with sharp eyes behind as snipers. They have a tough job. If they don't do it well, the troops may be overtaken and destroyed. If they do it too well for too long, they can't rejoin their own outfit and may be captured. Our men caught such a sniper. He had killed one of us, and men who fight beside each other are like brothers.

I was the battalion intelligence officer, and the sniper was brought back to me. I knew what the rules were. He was a prisoner of war. I should have immediately said something like, "Take the son of a bitch back to regiment."

But I hesitated, and in that pause the buddy of the man who had been killed shot the sniper. We searched the dead man's pockets. Inside were pictures of the wife and children he would never see because I had hesitated.

In life, as in the wilderness, as I would learn a decade later with Glen Canyon, you must know the situation you are in and act in time.

You don't forget something like that easily. I prefer to remember what happened two nights after we received word that World War II was over. My battalion became part of a regimental combat team that was told to go from Lake Garda to Passo de Resia on the Austrian border. When night fell beyond Merano, we turned on blackout lights from habit. But blackout lights don't light anything up worth a damn. I got a bright idea, and called on the radio to our commanding officer. This was Lt. Col. John Hay, who later would become a four-star general.

"Jack, why are we driving blackout? The war is over."

The colonel came back, "You got a point, Dave," and gave the command, "Turn on your lights, men."

They did, all along the four-mile column.

Our scouts found out that the Germans on the pass didn't know the war was over. Their artillery was laid on us, and they were about to fire when we lit up. Assuming that we knew something that they didn't know, they held their fire. They understood what the sudden turning on of our lights meant: that the war was over. I proclaimed myself a hero for having suggested that we turn our lights on.

The war against the Earth should also be over. It is time that we turn on the lights globally.

AS A FORMER military officer and a current observer of our amusing species, I am not so disingenuous as to believe that armed force will not be needed to police the errant of the world at least until Paradise arrives in the arms of Ecotopia and Sin has finally left the planet. Nevertheless, the Cold War has wound down, and there are some big armies out there, America's included. They have the technical know-how, the training, and the dedication to service needed to redesign human systems and restore natural systems—our ecological capital. What to do, now that peace has broken out?

And what, as well, to motivate inner-city youth? General Alfred Gray, former commandant of the U.S. Marine Corps, believes, "The greatest threat to national security is the combination of crime, drugs, lost educational opportunities, and the economic consequences of these failures." The army of the unemployed and a land badly in need of shoulder-to-shoulder restoring should be introduced to each other.

Recently, my eye caught some lines from Stewart Brand, the former military officer who gave us the original *Whole Earth Catalog*: "My platoon could have made short work of restoring a salmon stream, assisting a controlled forest burn, helping protect African wildlife from poachers, or planting native shrubs at the edge of a growing desert. I wonder if they might get this opportunity."

Brand adds: "Natural systems are priceless in value and nearly impossible to replace, but they're cheap to maintain. All you have to do is defend them."

Increasingly, intelligent and dedicated military men the world over are concluding, as has Brigadier Michael Harbottle, OBE, a former senior officer of NATO, that "the environment probably poses the greatest threat to the security and to the survival of the human race."

I alluded earlier to Robert D. Kaplan's strong conclusion in "The Coming Anarchy," printed last year in the *Atlantic Monthly*:

It is time to understand "the environment" for what it is: the national-security issue of the early twenty-first century. The political and strategic impact of surging populations, spreading disease, deforestation and soil erosion, water depletion, air pollution, and, possibly, rising sea levels in critical, overcrowded regions like the Nile Delta and Bangladesh—developments that will prompt mass migrations and, in turn, incite group conflicts—will be the core foreign-policy challenge from which most others will ultimately emanate.

Not only those remote regions, but Florida and California as well. I would add, with some hope, that anarchy need not reign. Deforestation, species extinction, soil erosion, water depletion, and air pollution are problems that environmentalists have had good solutions to for some time. The Earth can be healed. This is what restoration is all about. It is time for all policymakers to wake up.

Several years back, I generously offered the whole Pentagon building to an EPA audience: "If you add Restoration to your Protection mission, you will add more to global security than the Pentagon does." I haven't told the Pentagon yet.

The duty of armed forces is to serve their county. Our country, like most countries, is in danger from within, in the coming decades, from what we have done to ourselves, what we have destroyed. The Army Corps of Engineers once dammed and channelized our rivers with great skill. Remember the Kissimmee?

Industry required an end to the Everglades, or thought it did. It is time for army and Bureau of Reclamation engineers to restore our rivers instead of trickling and dribbling them, as a Native American puts it. I think, being good citizens, the engineers may well want to. Government should listen.

WHEN I MAKE speeches, I ask how many people in the audience would be willing to commit at least one year of their lives out of the next ten to working to restore the Earth. They could work for pay or as a volunteer, somewhere in the world, as close as the nearest mountain or the nearest poor urban area, as far away as the country of their dreams. Almost always, two-thirds of the audience raise their hands (I've asked almost 350,000 people so far). To demonstrate the vulnerability of polls, I ask the question again in a different way: How many would be unwilling? Rarely does a hand go up. "So it's unanimous," I tell them. "Let's go!"

People want to help, but there is no organization for them to join, certainly nothing coordinated on a global level that is dedicated to restoring the Earth, at least until our armies expand their role.

I am old enough to remember another corps: the Civilian Conservation Corps (CCC), under Franklin Roosevelt, during the Great Depression. It was particularly *un*-depressing to camp in the woods, shore up overgrazed stream banks, replant the prairies, and sleep around a campfire under a full moon (think of it: a full moon every twenty-eight days), or listen to the goose music overhead as you worked hard to save the geese. The CCC created forty-four wildlife refuges in this country and set 2 billion trees in the ground. Three million Americans were given jobs.

There should be an "Earth Corps" or perhaps a "CPR Corps" that would take up where the Peace Corps left off, and be fully concerned with endangered species and the endangered Earth. That's what Sam LaBudde proposed, in a moment between the campaign for dolphin-safe tuna and the equally successful campaign to stop drift-netters from strip-mining the high seas of fish.

A CPR Corps would help to solve the problem of the unemployed, but it would also enlist the highly employable. How many hydraulic engineers would truly love to jump the catwalk and restore rivers rather than build dams, perhaps even use their skills to rip out unnecessary dams, and get those salmon jumping again for joy? How many biologists might bolt the universities for a year, given the chance to show us all how it should be done? How many MBAs might welcome a chance, using intuition, to show what failure to invest in maintenance and replacement costs the Earth? Under a starry night sky, of course.

Our innovative scheme is to add a CPR component to other organizations, from the Peace Corps to the armed forces, from 3M to GM to the local ditch-digging company, from what is taught in kindergarten to what can be practiced in elder hostels, from regular columns in local papers to what a Bill Moyers can do on television, or what Bill Clinton can do if he stops being buffaloed by Republicans and gives us a series of eloquent fireside chats about what he will be doing for global CPR, that will give them, him, and us a chance.

No one budget can possibly pay for all the CPR the Earth so desperately needs. But with a certain sleight of hand, the funds can be found in already existing budgets of every government bureau and in each corporation, as well. CPR would be added to everybody's job description. That is, one of your finest duties would be to keep our life-support system alive, by restoring it. Call it a mandatory form of life insurance, like breathing and circulating your blood.

The CPR Corps, under various jurisdictions and as part of every budget, would work like an international Green Cross. Just as the Red Cross repairs the hurt and damage done to people in nature's wilder moments, the CPR Corps would bind the wounds and repair the damage people have done to the Earth.

Medically, CPR means cardiopulmonary resuscitation, getting the heart and lungs back in working order, with thump and mouth. That's what we need to do with the Earth: put it back in good order. Starting now.

The acronym CPR, you'll remember, stands for: Conservation, Preservation, and Restoration. I'd add Celebration, but it spoils the acronym.

You can sum it up with a ten-second sound bite: Conserve the golden eggs carefully. Preserve the goose or there will be no more golden eggs. If you've already damaged the goose, get going on restoration.

We would conserve by using our natural capital rationally. We haven't been all that reasonable lately. We would preserve what we cannot replace—the planet's biodiversity. If you can't replace something, then you'd better preserve it. Save all the parts. And we would restore by rebuilding, enlisting science and technology in generating rather than ripping apart the Earth's resources.

The one critical ingredient that has been missing is compassion. A CPR effort would build on compassion toward the Earth. And it will be fun.

The longer I've been here, the better I like this planet. We might just as well stop beating it, and get about healing the wounds no species but our own has inflicted.

CPR!

Restore!

CHAPTER 14

What Will It Cost?

> To move ahead to a restorative economy, the industrial
> corporations of the world must change to meet the world's
> needs, not the other way around.
>   —Paul Hawken

NATURALLY, people are worried about the taxing and
spending that will be required to pay the cost of restoring our
eco-structure, but we've been borrowing and spending ecological
capital—and deferring maintenance and replacement—since the
beginning of the Industrial Revolution. My idea of budgeting is
to ask, What will it cost if we don't do it? Once you pay to restore a forest or a river or a spot of blighted ground, you suddenly
understand how much it was worth in the first place. You're
much less likely to trash the Earth in the future.

In fact, once the idea of restoration takes hold, there is big
money to be made. If you don't think there is, try taking your car
to the shop, or your body to the doctor, and find out who's making money. You're glad to pay, too. Your car works better. You feel

better and will live longer. The Earth is not so different. There is something fundamentally wrong with treating the planet as if it were a business in liquidation.

Riparian restorations in and about California's cities sometimes cost $6,000 or more an acre. It is always cheaper to imagine what the cost to the Earth will be before we pollute, but those who are paid to clean up society's messes pay taxes, buy groceries, and vote, too, just like defense workers. The Southern Pacific Railroad, to its credit, spent millions to clean up the Sacramento River after a tank car full of herbicide derailed in the mountains near Dunsmuir. Hard-rock mining companies, which in this country often receive a free ride—or giveaway—from the antiquated 1872 Mining Law, can, should, and sometimes do tax themselves to reclaim the lands they destroy in the process of providing our gold jewelry and chrome, as well as more central metals.

There is also big money to be saved, once you understand how to solve the problem before it starts. In *The Ecology of Commerce*, my friend Paul Hawken, who founded Smith & Hawken, describes a delightful achievement of the 3M Company:

> To move ahead to a restorative economy, the industrial corporations of the world must change to meet the world's needs, not the other way around.... In 1975, Joseph Ling, head of 3M's environmental department, developed a program called Pollution Prevention Pays (3P),

the first integrated, intracompany approach to designing out pollution from manufacturing processes. The plan created incentives for the technical staff to modify product manufacturing methods so as to prevent hazardous and toxic waste, and to reduce costs. By reformulating products, changing processes, redesigning equipment, and recovering waste for reuse or recycling, 3M has been able to save $537 million. During the fifteen-year period, it reduced its air pollution by 120,000 tons, its wastewater by one billion gallons, its solid waste by 410,000 tons. Over 3,000 separate initiatives have contributed to the cause, and the key to the whole enterprise was a strong mandate from the top management of the corporation, linked with on-going support and assistance to line employees. In 1986, 3M expanded the scope of the program with a goal to eliminate 90 percent of all emissions by the end of this decade, and to achieve zero emissions sometime after that. Not only does this prevent material from entering the waste stream, it garners sales and therefore income for what was once an expense.

Paul has another idea for restoration from the start. Let Sony, for instance, retain title to the TV it leases or sells you, and have the company take it back when it stops working. No one could possibly know better how to disassemble it, reuse the reusable parts, and properly dispose of the toxic ones. In due course, the companies would learn to design the way nature does in nature's cradle-to-cradle scheme. Everything must be recyclable: TVs, refrigerators, cars, all goods currently disposable.

The 3M Company did the right thing by the Earth. The problem of the corporation, especially the multinational, is that it is given the rights of a person without conscience. Somehow, we've got to build conscience back into the corporate structure. When I say "we," I mean consumers, customers, executives, stockholders, and employees. Corporations have the organizational ability. They have the money. They have the political power. But they've got to realize that there will be no corporations, no stockholders, no profits, and no sex on a dead planet. The Fortune 500 must be brought into the restoration movement. Otherwise, it won't happen. Time is running out, fast.

Those corporate directors who understand that their grandchildren will live on the Earth after them have already made the U-turn. Green business is big, and getting much bigger. I am always heartened by companies such as Ben & Jerry's, The Body Shop, Esprit, Interface Inc., Patagonia, Real Goods, Smith & Hawken, and 3M, and their often much larger counterparts in Europe. There is such a thing as the consumer vote, as the writers of economic textbooks are so fond of citing. It should be wielded with vigilance by environmentalists, who must understand who is doing what to the Earth, and buy accordingly. When that is apparent, things have a way of changing overnight. Those dolphin-catching tuna companies changed, and so did Nestlé, Gallo,

Burger King, and McDonald's, in their various experiments with Styrofoam containers, rain-forest beef, and pesticides. Many other corporations might enjoy the consumer support that the public's embrace of restoration and right-living will bring, as well as corrective subsidies.

As a small spur to progress, I would like to publish a book with the title, *The Misfortune 500*. Each page would have a picture of what a misdirected company had done to the Earth, a before-and-after illustration. However, since corporations all over the world are now making that U-turn, the book would have two parts, and it would be reissued every two years. The good companies effecting change would move up front, until the back of the book grew thinner and thinner. Finally, the back section would contain just one blank, white page.

That would be my idea of a good read.

CHAPTER 15

The Cure for What Ails Us

I seek acquaintance with nature—to know her moods and
manners. Primitive nature is the most interesting to me.
I take infinite pains to know all the phenomena of spring,
for instance, thinking that I have here the entire poem, and
then, to my chagrin, I learn that it is but an imperfect copy
that I possess and have read, that my ancestors have torn out
many of the first leaves and grandest passages, and mutilated
it in many places. I should not like to think that some demigod
had come before me and picked out some of the best of the
stars. I wish to know an entire heaven and an entire Earth.

—Henry David Thoreau, *Journals*, March 23, 1856

ONLY A FEW years ago, I was flying nonstop from
Kuwait to Los Angeles. At one point I was bored, because it
was cloudy and I could not see below. To pass the hours—I was
really bored—I counted the number of times I chewed my airplane lunch.

It took 2,000 chews. On a later flight, this time from Tokyo
to New York nonstop, I was bored again, and decided to count
the chews involved in dinner, about 4,000. I was not awake
enough to count the number of times I chewed at breakfast, but
I'll throw in an arbitrary 1,000. That is 7,000 chews a day. This

concentration on an act we take for granted set about a whole chain reaction of thinking.

What happens when we chew? Each time, the softest tissue you can touch, the tip of your tongue, has to take food and roll it on both sides into the path of the hardest tissue you've got, your tooth enamel, and then get the hell out of the way before you bite.

Every now and then you bite your tongue and then you're sorry, but it's very rare. I haven't bitten mine in years. It's a very careful tongue—when I eat.

You are reading this book with the 120 million rods and cones in each of your two retinas. Those cones and rods have been installed in just the right way. You see these pages—you see creation—in 3-D. That is, each eye receives a different picture and your brain puts it together. Do you object? No, this is the space with which you see the world. This is the space between us.

If you looked at a diagram of the human ear, you would think that it's just too complicated to work. If you looked at a transparent model of a human being, and the intricate folds of nervous and circulatory systems, you'd say that they cannot possibly work, either.

My friend Alan Nixon, former president of the American Chemical Society, told me that the human body can carry out 100,000 different chemical reactions. Fortunately, you don't have to run your reactions or nervous or circulatory system. You don't have to worry about your ears, or whether your tongue will get out of the way when you bite. The food you had will be distributed to the trillions of cells in your body. The system goes on. If we had to think about it, we'd probably screw up.

I get a little excited talking about these things, what I call the wildness within. It's my "Gee whiz!" factor: *The whole immune system, incredible!* Of course, you're especially impressed if you've been kept more or less intact for eighty-seven years.

We don't know how most of this is done, but our bodies do. What else has been passed along the genetic train that we haven't yet realized? Why do we have intuition? Intuition is quite important. It reminds you to be frightened when you may be too stunned to remember why.

These autopilot systems remind me of the colony of leaf-cutting ants in Professor E.O. Wilson's office at Harvard. Wilson likes ants, and probably knows more about them than anyone else. He showed me the colony at work. He put some leaves, which were about half the size of your hand, into a plastic box. The colony and the plastic food box were joined with a small branch. The ants cut the leaves into little pieces and brought them to their nest. Inside the nest they had a retinue of smaller ants that belonged to the same colony. The littler ants took the leaf pieces and cut them into smaller pieces. Then still smaller ants took them below to feed the fungi, which become the food they take to the young. This is one of the best examples of sustainable agriculture going. They also carry the ant poop to a greater depth, which enriches the soil.

Professor Wilson said, "Watch this," and rapped on the glass of the nest. Up from the chaos of debris came the warriors, three times the size of the larger workers, their mandibles capable of cutting leather. If I could understand ant language, I might have heard them ask, "What's wrong up here?" Finding nothing wrong, they went below to resume goofing off.

The weight of all the ants on the Earth happens to be greater than the weight of all of us. These little ants do not like clear-cutting, they don't use herbicides, they don't like our pesticides or chemical fertilizers. And informed by chemical signals from the queen, they know exactly what they're doing.

They are as well instructed as the arctic tern, a bird that migrates from pole to pole. The young of the arctic tern begin their long migration before the parents do, so you can see what good maps they are born with. It now occurs to me that the arctic tern isn't that good. If you start from the North Pole, south is the only direction there is, so how could you get lost? It's harder for the monarch butterfly. East of the Rockies, monarchs from Canada and the U.S. go to Mexico for the winter, to one little piece of forest, where the right trees are. West of the Rockies, they go to Pacific Grove, California. No parent guides them. Their genes carry flawless maps.

These are just a few of the miracles of wildness we're getting rid of without even knowing what we are eliminating. As Noel Brown, director of the United Nations Environment Programme once put it, we may have already destroyed the cure for AIDS. How much of the pharmacological basis underlying modern medicine is rooted, literally, in forest plants, for instance? As Jay Hair of the National Wildlife Federation tells it, when his daughter was three, her doctor said, "She has four days to live." Today she is in graduate school. The medicine that cured her disease came from the rosy periwinkle, which grew only on the island of Madagascar and is now extinct.

We need to tire of trashing wildness. It's not making us happy. It's not making us healthy. It is making us miserable and despairing. Killing trees, habitat, and animals, and separating ourselves from nature is making us all a bit crazy. We need to restore the Earth because we need to save the wild. We need to save the wild in order to save ourselves.

AS HUMANS, we have the ability to feel compassion, to love, to reproduce, to think, to avoid annihilation. How did we acquire our wildness within? How did this magic come about?

The minimum genetic material required to build and operate all the human beings who have ever lived on Earth, about 100 billion of us, would fit into a sphere one-sixth of an inch in diameter. All the messages as to where the rods and cones should go, the development of our minds, conscious and unconscious, were developed over the last three and a half billion years, through trial and error, through success and failure, through symbiosis. We all still possess a little fragment of the first bit of life on Earth. Consequently, everything that's alive is related—and a submicroscopic part of us all is three and a half billion years old. Some of us show that age more than others.

But how did this miracle happen? What shaped it? It wasn't civilization because there wasn't any. It was something else. It was wilderness. Because that's all there was.

As Nancy Newhall said, wilderness is the ultimate encyclopedia, holding the answers to questions that we have not yet learned how to ask. Yet with our technology, and for short-term jobs, or out of greedlock, or simply from not understanding what is happening, we are obliterating what little wilderness we have left.

There have been many evolutionary failures. Millions upon millions of species are no longer here. Evolution did them in. But *we* are here, *you* are here.

So why should we insist on wiping out species a thousand times faster than evolution did—when that malpractice might easily wipe us out?

Every species that is lost diminishes our environment, the Earth. When we do this to ourselves, it degrades us and lessens our chance of there being a human future. There will be no joy in being almost ancestors.

If we are to restore our natural capital, then we must have examples of the true wild to work from. How shall we figure the future out, how shall we be able to help ourselves, if we find we have paved, logged, polluted, burned, and condominiumized the templates? Burning books is something most of us don't like to do. It worries us when it happens. We should be annoyed, like Thoreau a century and a half ago, at people who are playing demigod by tearing out the pages of the poem that is the Earth, and mutilating the best passages.

That poem contains us.

PART IV

Wildness

CHAPTER 16

Where the Wilderness Is

In wildness is the preservation of the world.
— Henry David Thoreau

IN WILDNESS is the preservation of the world. I liked that line so much when I was executive director of the Sierra Club that I used it for the title of a Thoreau anthology, illustrated with photographs by Eliot Porter. The book, quite expensive, was third in the club's exhibit-format series. If you just looked at the floating autumn leaves on the cover and that title, *"In Wildness Is the Preservation of the World,"* you would get the message. My wife said nobody would buy a book with such a title. So far, a million people have.

When you lose contact with wildness, you've lost an important part of yourself. I think it makes people sad, without their even knowing why, deep down. Wildness is also a fairly good control of hubris. When you understand how recent an arrival we are, in comparison with a forest or a mountain, and you begin to understand how much wildness contributed to making us as a successful evolutionary project, you acquire some humility.

It is not hard to imagine a society that has lost its wilderness. Too much of Europe is such a place. China is such a place. Sometimes, I wonder if that loss leads to things like the Tiananmen Square massacre in 1989. Is it possible that our more arrogant tendencies run rampant, like scared rabbits, in the absence of wilderness?

A river like the North Fork of the Flathead, Tom McGuane wrote in 1994, "ought to go through South-Central Los Angeles" because of the calming effect it might have. That is a teasing thought. "The average American," McGuane continues, "is two-thirds river water and ought to have more sense about these things than he has shown. Obviously, a creature that is itself made mostly of rivers would do well to offer itself to the exaltation of rivers in good works and ceremonial acts of worship like fishing and contemplative floating in poetic watercraft such as canoes and jonboats."

Something called the Los Angeles River still runs in Los Angeles, but in a concrete channel and only now and then. It does not calm Los Angeles.

Neither Los Angeles nor a bonsai is a good substitute for wilderness.

THE GALÁPAGOS Islands contain wildness for which there is no substitute. Anne and I were delighted to discover that you could still walk among basking seals without their moving away, or among frigate birds, and that birds saw fit to land on us. Certainly, I never expected to be courted by a blue-footed booby, and briefly thought I was until I moved myself out of her way so she could court a creature bluer footed than I.

Nevertheless, I concluded that our own major wilderness areas in North America are wilder than anything in the Galápagos, although our wildlife will never be as untroubled by people. Our wilderness will remain wilder so long as we stop chopping away at it. That said, let's remember that only about 4 percent of the United States is designated wilderness, and half of this is in Alaska. Loopholes abound in the legal language protecting these remnants, and each generation must review the gems left it by the generation before, and be ready to guard the house against burglars. The well-traveled Sierra and the lonely Bob Marshall Wilderness in Montana, according to an army study for World War II, are the only two places in the Lower Forty-eight where you can get more than ten miles away from a road.

But what exquisite places.

Bob Marshall—he hated to be called anything but plain Bob—was the wild conscience of the second Roosevelt Administration. We have a wilderness system in America in large part because of Bob, who once wrote a reply to a woman who insisted on calling him Mr. Marshall: "When you call me Mr. Marshall it makes me feel so thoroughly miserable I want to knock my head against the side of a house." I met him only once, but I always admired his uncompromising stance. He wrote, there is but "one hope of repulsing the tyrannical ambition of civilization to conquer every niche on the whole Earth. That hope is the organization of spirited people who will fight for the freedom of wilderness."

Bob formed the Wilderness Society with Aldo Leopold and others, such as Benton MacKaye. They are great Americans, great citizens of the Earth, and should be recognized as such, along with Howard Zahniser, who wrote the definition of wilderness that is now the law: "A wilderness, in contrast with those areas where man and his own works dominate the landscape, is hereby recognized as an area where the Earth and its community of life are untrammeled by man, where man himself is a visitor who does not remain."

To me, a wilderness is where the flow of wildness is essentially uninterrupted by technology; without wilderness, the world's a cage. To Mrs. Malaprop, it is where the hand of man has not set foot. To Bob Marshall, if you set foot in it, you shouldn't be able to cross it unless you sleep out. It would have to be that big. Take your choice, and remember that there is no better place to rediscover the wildness the ages have made perfect—and beyond that, there are still stars out there to make the night friendly. When did you last see the stars?

Aldo Leopold was one of the first to counsel, "Think like a mountain." He wrote: "Man always kills the thing he loves, and so we the pioneers have killed our wilderness. Some say we had to. Be that as it may, I am glad I shall never be young without wild country to be young in. Of what avail are forty freedoms without a blank spot on the map?"

CHAPTER 17

Listening to Mountains

Flocks of birds have flown high and away.
A solitary drift of cloud, too, has gone, wandering on.
And I sit alone with the Ching-Ting Peak, towering beyond.
We never grow tired of each other, the mountain and I.

—Li Po

I CLIMBED many mountains between 1930 and 1956, and I keep climbing them in my dreams. I have never considered it to be a victory to stand alone or with my companions on the mountaintop. That is not the right way to view what has happened after a successful ascent. The mountain merely relaxed for a moment. I didn't beat the mountain, but I did earn it.

The thrill of helicoptering up to virgin powder in order to ski trackless snow has spread from Aspen to Alaska. But it seems to me that it takes the earning out of skiing. I believe in cross-country skis, not snowmobiles. I hate to see the challenge diminished.

What you've earned, you are glad you've got. You put part of yourself into getting it. It is not spoon-fed. And people who believe there are getting to be too many restrictions in wilderness areas need to get out and organize for more wilderness.

We certainly need it. When I climbed Shiprock in 1937, when I earlier made the attempt on Mount Waddington in 1935, there were fewer than 1,000 climbers in the country. Now we have about 250,000. Today we have indoor climbing gymnasiums, and outside we are beginning to damage the mountains themselves. I did it myself, with those pitons and expansion bolts I used on Shiprock.

Today there are something like 6,000 or 7,000 expansion bolt holes in Yosemite Valley alone. This worries me. Some of the perpetrators say that their expansion bolts are only used for safety. If so, fine. But if they are being used for ego, not safety, that is another thing entirely.

"Ego bolts" are employed in order to find a new way up a cliff that could not otherwise be climbed. Climbers sometimes put in the bolts with a battery-powered portable drill as they rappel, then they use the bolts to make the ascent. I think this demeans mountaineering.

It's like anything else. As long as you think there is an unlimited supply of something, then you think it will replace itself, if you think at all.

When I was climbing, there were so few people yet so many cliffs. We didn't think we could ever bother those cliffs. When we came upon a crack on the mountain that had vegetation, we would dig it out. We called this gardening. When you climb a tough mountain, you want to stand on solid rock, not on a flower or on moss. We would just toss the garden over the edge.

Today there aren't so many alpine gardens left. Today we've also got the white cliffs of Yosemite, because so many people are assiduously chalking hands to make them hold better.

If young climbers need to do these things for protection, and don't damage the mountain, OK. But if they cannot make the top without damaging the mountain, then I say, try something else. Skydiving. Windsurfing. Hang gliding. Ping-Pong. Let the mountain be.

LOREN EISELEY suggested that rocks and mountains just move more slowly than we do, so slowly that we can't understand their motion very well. Loren explained more than mountains to me in person and in books. He wrote, "We are compounded of dust and the light of a star." What power in so few words!

François Matthes provided scientific detail. He talked about the tracks that rocks will leave on a slope. Imagine a slope. The sun rises. The rock warms, expands, and moves infinitesimally upward, perpendicular to the slope. The sun sets. The rock cools, and moves infinitesimally but vertically down, with gravity. That works out to be a daily tiny triangle. The track it leaves can be measured in the lichen. It takes a long time for the lichen to grow back, maybe fifty or a hundred years. Slowly, you see, the rock makes its mark. Of course, some rocks move faster, like the big block I pulled out climbing the Thumb in the Sierra in 1933. Miraculously, I avoided falling with it.

I believe that mountains should accept natural deterioration, because that's in their destiny. But I don't think we should mess them up. We've messed up enough things, besides mountains, to last us for several more civilizations. There are better sports than that.

LET THE MOUNTAINS talk. The mountains first talked to me through poets I had to read in junior high English. Longfellow first:

> This is the forest primeval.
> The murmuring pines and the hemlocks,
> Bearded with moss, and in garments green, indistinct
>   in the twilight,
> Stand like Druids of eld, with voices sad and prophetic. . . .

I could hear what was happening in Sir Walter Scott's lead to *The Lady of the Lake*:

> The stag at eve had drunk his fill,
> Where danced the moon on Monan's rill,
> And deep his midnight lair had made
> In lone Glenartney's hazel shade.

Thoreau came much later, when in *Walden* he told how to get where you can hear mountains talk:

Rise free from care before the dawn and seek adventures. Let the noon find you by other lakes and the night overtake thee everywhere at home. . . . Let the thunder rumble. . . .

Soon I would hear the talk directly. Not too sonorously from the thunder, cascading water, or falling stone, but musically enough from the jay's complaint, the kookaburra's laugh, the coyote's howl, pines answering the wind, fallen leaves answering your shuffling feet, and the lilting notes of a stream, hermit thrush, or canyon wren completing the symphony.

Twelve centuries earlier, Li Po wrote of what I can hear with my spirit:

Flocks of birds have flown high and away.
A solitary drift of cloud, too, has gone, wandering on.
And I sit alone with the Ching-Ting Peak, towering beyond.
We never grow tired of each other, the mountain and I.

I believe we should listen eloquently. Try still harder and you may find that all your senses can talk to you. You handicap yourself if you don't let them.

Not everybody is able to climb real mountains, of course, whether or not they try hard. That probably must apply to me.

For all its benefits, age can get in the way. How much access should be provided handicapped people—handicapped in the normal sense? I am thinking of a discussion we had when Franklin Roosevelt came to see the new national park, Kings Canyon, that he had helped us establish in the Sierra. Because of polio, he had to be lifted into his car. San Joaquin Valley officials wanted to construct a road into the new park so that he could be driven in. Will Colby, who was serving his half a century as Sierra Club secretary, said, "If we don't have that road, President Roosevelt won't be able to see the canyon."

We shouldn't have built that road, even for the president, but the commitment had been made. The road was built, though it was kept very short. I agree there should be a good sampling of things for handicapped people to experience. But if you make it easy for anybody to get into wilderness, it isn't wilderness any longer. Don't do it for me. I don't want it to be any easier for me to get to that place in Yosemite that is informally called Browers' Bench—if I want to go again, I'll simply have to get back in shape, or crawl.

I HAVEN'T DONE any serious climbing since 1956. The serious part that year was my decision to stop at the *bergschrund*, the highest crevasse on the glacier under the north face of the Grand Teton. I was older than my companions by thirteen and twenty-four years, respectively, and I didn't see why my handicap of age should be shared. So Dick Emerson, who became the outstanding mountaineer-ranging in the Tetons, and Phil Berry, who would twice be president of the Sierra Club, made the ascent. I learned to share the attitude expressed when Benton MacKaye told me, in his eighties, "I don't have to climb Katahdin anymore." Mount Katahdin, in Maine, is where the sun first hits the continental United States.

Like many somewhat older people who have enjoyed many somewhat strenuous sports, I had no thoughts that my mountaineering, that is, my difficult mountaineering, would end. Eight years ago I was in Florence, Italy, at a meeting of world-class climbers, who had climbed the Eigerwand solo, in winter. Unbelievable! And there, in a slide show, was eighty-six-year-old Fritz Wiesner, doing a 5.11 (a harder climb, on the mountaineers' scale, than I would like to dream of climbing).

That shook me. I announced that I was going home to Berkeley, getting in shape, getting the right shoes, and getting back on a rock. Well, I got back to Berkeley, but so far I haven't even got the right shoes.

CHAPTER 18

Rachel Carson's Pelicans

The pelican remembers the cone from which the first
redwood fell.
        —Robinson Jeffers

A LITTLE WHILE ago, I was counting brown pelicans
and remembering Rachel Carson.

I was sitting in Sinbad's Restaurant on the San Francisco
waterfront, as I have off and on for twenty-five years, waiting
patiently for my poached salmon to arrive. The pelicans were putting on a show as they glided under the Bay Bridge, then dropped
to coast low and long on their bow waves. Sometimes from my
table at Sinbad's I count five or six pelicans, sometimes many
more. My record for one day is 176, which includes lunch and
happy hour. Pelicans are among the biggest birds in North
America, the brown a little smaller than the white, which has a
ten-foot wingspread. My empathy is with the browns, the ones
almost put out of business by DDT.

No one likes pelicans better than I do. Rachel Carson also liked pelicans, and did a great deal to save them, beginning with her book, *Silent Spring*, in 1962, which awakened the world and shook me, too. Rachel explained how DDT weakened the shells of pelicans' eggs, and the eggs of many other birds. Spring in America was becoming as silent as winter. Barely measurable amounts of insecticide could impair cell functions, such as reproduction. Rachel made it clear that living cells, whether in birds, insects, or humans, had important elements in common. What we did to end a function in insects could have a boomerang effect we might not like. That truth has not sunk in far enough yet. We may discover that industry is giving us a quicker life through chemistry—and it will take chemists to save us.

In the late 1960s, my family and I visited Eliot Porter on his family's island, Great Spruce Head, in Penobscot Bay, Maine. On an islet in a channel was a tree with a nest. Sitting on the nest was a female osprey. Around the island were other trees with nests abandoned by ospreys who could not make their DDT-damaged eggs hatch. Flying in from the water came the male osprey. As we watched, he hovered, and the female flew off the nest to join him in midair. They seemed almost to confer. Then they just went away together, abandoning that nest and the hopeless eggs. It just wasn't working. DDT had ended the life in them. Anne and I shared the ospreys' grief.

Rachel's book led to the banning of DDT, at least in the United States, but banning has not reduced its persistence, and unscrupulous chemical companies still manufacture the compound elsewhere, inhibiting restoration and who knows what else.

PELICANS AND Rachel Carson are linked, for me, and I remember the last time I saw her. She asked me to help her see the redwoods in Muir Woods. Anne and our daughter, Barbara, became the friendly native guides, joined by a National Park Service guide, with a wheelchair for Rachel. She had come to California for a conference. Terminal cancer could not prevent her from working.

From Muir Woods we drove to the shore at Fort Cronkhite, now part of the Golden Gate National Recreation Area. In the lagoon just inland were perhaps fifty brown pelicans having a hell of a good time, perhaps celebrating the beginning of their recovery with a pelican ballet, on that sunny day. I have to believe in magic, for what else could have led those pelicans to know that Rachel Carson would have preferred them to redwoods?

I DON'T KNOW how much money the chemical industry invested in trying and failing to discredit Rachel Carson. It must be proprietary information. So far, we hear, they are putting up $15 million to discredit Theo Colburn, the Rachel Carson reincarnate, and her associates, who are coming up with a most alarming message about the silent toxic sea of artificial estrogens polluting our water as DDT once did the land. Chemistry, in the natural process of our evolution, is self-controlling. In less experienced hands, it is producing uncounted, perhaps uncountable, products nature cannot handle, nor can we.

The things Rachel warned about nearly forty years ago reformed the environmental movement, but the public is forgetting. What the chemical industry is now trying to silence, we are forced to infer, is Theo Colburn's new message—the chemical assault on the male. Especially the human male. This half of humanity, which is still running most of the chemical industry (and government), is likely to become effectively concerned about what certain chemicals, odorless, colorless, and tasteless but not timeless, can do to the sperm and its distribution system—especially when we apply these chemicals without knowing what we are doing or how many generations it will affect. Like the human egg, the sperm knows the facts of life and shouldn't be decimated, or worse, have two heads and no tail.

So if you see chemical industry ads and articles by indentured scientists that say everything is OK, prepare to accept them the same way you accept the tobacco industry's assurances that smoking, first- and second-hand, is no problem.

Listen carefully to Theo. Remember Rachel.

WHILE THE PELICANS outside Sinbad's glided past, I also thought about condors. The salmon and hollandaise were trying to get together in the kitchen, and Chardonnay was my solace. In that morning's paper, July 7, 1994, I had read a short article from the Associated Press:

California Condor Back in Captivity

A California condor in Los Angeles has been returned to captivity because it did not adapt to life in the wild. The male condor, hatched in a zoo program to rebuild the wild population of the endangered birds, was one of two who flew back to civilization. He was captured Monday.

A condor is about 5 percent feathers, blood, and bone, and about 95 percent place. Place designs the condor, as it does the arctic tern and the monarch butterfly. A condor must learn to know the wind, where to find food and water, where to nest, where to hang out. A young condor remains at the nest for a year, and accompanies its parents for another five, a little like a human child—but how the condor can fly!

I was seventy-two before I saw my first condor, and what an extraordinary creature it was! Stable as a 747, feathering the wind with just the tips of its primaries, soaring and rising higher and higher on a convenient thermal, then gliding on and on and on and out of sight without flapping a wing. How lazy can you get?

Thirty years ago, there was a big argument, of which I was a part, of how best to save the condor. Take it out of the wild and raise it in a captive breeding program, or leave it where it is and protect its habitat. With the condor, I said, if you want to save the species, you must save the place. That may not be true for all birds, but that is the law for the condor.

We lost the argument. The biologists wanted an interesting and well-funded program they would get to manage. The Audubon Society thought it might work. The owners of the large tracts of coastal Californian land that comprised the condors' habitat wanted to develop their lands. I could understand that last part. Who was going to compensate the owners for the loss of their lands, just because condors had always lived there?

Today people still push captive-breeding programs instead of habitat protection. Sometimes captive-breeding works. Other times it is a device for getting a creature out of the way.

When my salmon finally arrived before me at Sinbad's, I had mixed emotions. I was glad to see lunch. I missed Rachel Carson. I missed the condors. And I was glad the pelicans would be back, same time, same place, but different and abundant, another day.

CHAPTER 19

Neat Tricks

IT IS FUN to discover how nature works, to find
out, for example, that humans have to make cement at 1,800
degrees Fahrenheit, while a hen can make stronger cement at 103
degrees, and a clam can do still better at the temperature of sea-
water. What's the trick? We still don't know. If we found out,
would we pave everything in sight?

Other neat tricks: The bombardier beetle produces actual
steam in an internal chamber and fires it at its enemies. Another
beetle modifies the surface tension of water with a detergent that
sinks water skaters for an easy meal. Another beetle can inject a
frog with a chemical that liquefies everything inside the frog's
skin, and then has a drink. (The U.S. Department of Defense
should not be told about this until it firmly commits to restoration.)

There's all this exciting stuff! We haven't spoiled it all, and have only begun to learn about it. With vision, we can spare what's left.

Allow me to offer you a short course in ecology, beginning with rot. Rot is an extraordinarily important process. Rot is highly exciting. But we give it a three-letter word. We say, "This tree is sick," and "This is rotten, anyway. We should get rid of it."

By removing the rotten tree from the forest, we knock out of existence all the species that were going to use that tree for a home, for their dinner, until it rotted away completely, and helped to nourish the next tree, maybe 200 or more years down the line. This is a very good system. Unfortunately, we've learned to interrupt it rather than to live with it. We have learned how to break the circle of life instead of respecting it.

Nature recycles everything. There isn't anything that isn't recycled. Go outside. Look at the natural systems. Study them and learn to read the Earth. You will see what it has had time to learn. You will begin to understand the life force.

"The cold smokeless fires of decay"—which are what rot is— require energy. I may be wrong in this, but I believe there's a little surplus everywhere in nature. We may live on some of that surplus, but we must not take so much that we destroy the system.

My apple tree will produce a whole bunch of apples, and if I don't mistreat it, it will probably last far longer than I will. Apple trees live almost 100 years. I'll use some while I can, but none will be unused. All that time, those half-eaten apples that the squirrels let fall to the ground will feed other species. There are far more apples than the apple tree needed just to reproduce itself, or for me to make applesauce from.

Part of the recycling of nature is to make sure that the other forms of life that are necessary to their own recycling circles are fed along the way. Life is a circle of nourishment. Some might call it inefficient, but they would be wrong. The natural law, hard to explain, is that efficiency and stability are incompatible.

What is a tree really up to? What is a tree about? It locks up carbon. If that carbon gets buried by floods and mud, and begins to collect downstream, it begins to form the beginnings of the fossil fuel inventory available for whatever, or to whomever, centuries from now. That's recycling. The carbon is taken out of the system for a while.

That is only part of what is happening. Most of this change takes place above ground. While it is alive, the tree frees oxygen as well as locking up carbon. While all this green stuff is living on the surface of the Earth, we have the oxygen that it has made free. This is rather important for us, if we like breathing. That's why I have been saying that we have a large potential constituency, as environmentalists: those who like breathing. Or those who wish their great-grandchildren might breathe at all.

When we burn carbon for energy, we free carbon monoxide and dioxide. If we burn too much, we've got problems. Carbon monoxide kills, and we may well overload the carbon dioxide sink. That can change the fate of the biosphere, the fate of the Earth, us. This is called the greenhouse effect.

It does not have to be this way.

One-third of the energy that comes from the sun is reflected back to outer space, beyond our jurisdiction so far. Another third lifts water. It's a very nice system because it just lifts the good water. It leaves the salt and other ingredients behind. It was not nature's idea to put some things in the air to mix up with her clean water. These things dirty up the air, and acid rain develops. That was our idea, except for a volcano or two. Nature's idea was to lift up water and form clean raindrops and snowflakes.

Snow stores water very nicely. Are we trying to get rid of that benefit by bringing up the temperature of the Earth so that we no longer get snow? Snow is a fairly important form of water storage.

Then we realize that, to serve ourselves, we need to intercept that water. Some people who consider themselves really bright human beings consider that any water that flows to the sea is wasted. I believe that to be wasted thinking.

The unintercepted water that comes from the land brings nutrients and minerals that are terribly important for everything that lives in the ocean. We keep trying to interrupt that flow, through dams and diversions, and by dumping in things that nature can't handle.

The commercials on television tell you the oven cleaner will just clean your oven. You spray the chemical on and everything you don't like disappears. But it doesn't disappear when you flush it down the drain. It moves toward the ocean and it kills. What systems does it destroy that ultimately are used to build our own bodies? The Earth knows how to recycle mountains safely. It may gag on oven cleaner. Oven cleaner removes grease, and may ultimately remove you.

Enjoy watching nature at work. The sun lifts the water. The water washes the mountains down. Then the tectonic plates say, "Oh, no, you don't!" and push the mountains back up. That's long-term recycling. Water is very good at taking mountains apart. If it weren't for the tectonic plates, the world would be flat by now. So be grateful for tectonic plates. Keep them moving! Except if you live in Los Angeles.

PART V

Saving the Earth

CHAPTER 20

The Third Planet: Operating Instructions

TECTONIC PLATES are maintenance-free, or are they?

The first edition of *Let the Mountains Talk* was written for Earth Day 1995, the twenty-fifth anniversary of Earth Day. Twenty-five years ago I wrote an endpaper for the *New York Times Magazine*, with the title, "The Third Planet: Operating Instructions." The *Reader's Digest* reprinted the endpaper, and then it became a booklet. More than 18 million copies got around. But I am a little worried we've misplaced the instructions again. They need restoring. Here they are, for a new generation and a new Earth Day.

THIS PLANET *has been delivered wholly assembled and in perfect working condition, and is intended for fully automatic and trouble-free operation in orbit around its star, the Sun.*

However, to ensure proper functioning, all passengers are requested to familiarize themselves fully with the following instructions. Loss or even temporary misplacement of these instructions may result in calamity. Passengers who must proceed without the benefit of these rules are likely to cause considerable damage before they can learn the proper operating procedures for themselves.

Components

It is recommended that passengers become completely familiar with the following planetary components:

1. *Air*. The air accompanying this planet is not replaceable. Enough has been supplied to cover the land and the water, but not very deeply. In fact, if the atmosphere were reduced to the density of water, then it would be a mere 33 feet deep. In normal use, the air is self-cleaning. It may be cleaned in part if excessively soiled. The passengers' lungs will be of help—up to a point. However, they will discover that anything they throw, spew, or dump into the air will return to them in due course. Since passengers will need to use the air, on the average, every five seconds, they should treat it accordingly.

2. *Water*. The water supplied with this planet isn't replaceable either. The operating water supply is very limited: if the Earth were the size of an egg, all the water on it would fit into a single drop. The water contains many creatures, almost all of which eat and may be eaten; these creatures may be eaten by

human passengers. If disagreeable things are dispersed in the planet's water, however, caution should be observed, since the water creatures concentrate the disagreeable things in their tissues. If human passengers eat the water creatures, they will add disagreeable things to their diet. In general, passengers are advised not to disdain water, which is what they mostly are.

3. *Land.* Although the surface of the planet is varied and seems abundant, only a small amount of land is suited to growing things, and that essential part should not be misused. It is also recommended that no attempt be made to disassemble the surface too deeply inasmuch as the land is supported by a molten and very hot underlying layer that will grow little but volcanoes.

4. *Life.* The foregoing components help make life possible. There is only one life per passenger, and it should be treated with dignity. Instructions covering the birth, operation and maintenance, and disposal for each living entity have been thoughtfully provided. These instructions are contained in a complex language, called the DNA code, which is not easily understood. However, this does not matter, as the instructions are fully automatic. Passengers are cautioned, however, that radiation and many dangerous chemicals can damage the instructions severely. If in any way living species are destroyed, or rendered unable to reproduce, the filling of reorders is subject to long delays.

5. *Fire.* This planet has been designed and fully tested at the factory for totally safe operation with fuel constantly transmitted from a remote source, the Sun, provided at absolutely no charge.

The following must be observed with greatest care: The planet comes with a limited reserve fuel supply, contained in fossil deposits, which should be used only in emergencies. Use of this reserve fuel supply entails hazards, including the release of certain toxic metals, which must be kept out of the air and the food supply of living things. The risk will not be appreciable if the use of the emergency fuel is extended over the operating life of the planet. Rapid use, if sustained only for a brief period, may produce unfortunate results.

Maintenance

The kinds of maintenance will depend upon the number and constituency of the passengers. If only a few million human passengers wish to travel at a given time, no maintenance will be required, and no reservations will be necessary. The planet is self-maintaining, and the external fuel source will provide exactly as much energy as is needed or can be safely used. However, if a very large number of people insist on boarding at one time, serious problems will result, requiring costly solutions.

Operation

Barring extraordinary circumstances, it is necessary only to observe the mechanism periodically and to report any irregularities to the Smithsonian Institution. However, if owing to misuse of the planet's mechanism, observations show a substantial change in the predictable patterns of sunrise and sunset, passengers should prepare to leave the vehicle.

Emergency Repairs

If, through no responsibility of the current passengers, damage to the planet's operating mechanisms has been caused by ignorant or careless action of the previous travelers, it is best to request the Manufacturer's assistance (best obtained through prayer).

Upon close examination, this planet will be found to consist of complex and fascinating detail in design and structure. Some passengers, upon discovering these details in the past, have attempted to replicate or improve the design and structure, or have even claimed to have invented them. The Manufacturer, having among other things invented the opposable thumb, may be amused by this. It is reliably reported that at this point, however, it appears to the Manufacturer that a full panoply of consequences of this thumb idea will not be without an element of unwelcome surprise.

CHAPTER 21

Unwise Misuse

> As we lengthen and elaborate the chain of technology that
> intervenes between us and the natural world, we forget that
> we become steadily more vulnerable to even the slightest
> failure in that chain.
>
> —Paul B. Sears

WHEN MAURICE STRONG became the first head of the
United Nations Environment Programme, he told the following story:

> A fire broke out in a crowded theater. Everybody rose up
> and started for the exits. But the piano player, sensing the
> impending panic, promptly began to play the piano. He
> played so well, and with such nonchalance and assurance,
> that the audience returned to their seats—and burned to
> death.

Rush Limbaugh, the most popular critic of the environmental movement, plays the piano in his best-seller *The Way Things
Ought to Be*:

Mount Pinatubo in the Philippines spewed forth more than a thousand times the amount of ozone-depleting chemicals in one eruption than all the fluorocarbons manufactured by wicked, diabolical, and insensitive corporations in history. . . . Mankind can't possibly equal the output of even one eruption from Pinatubo, much less 4 billion years' worth of them, so how can we destroy the ozone?

Mr. Limbaugh considers those who worry about ozone and other environmental concerns to be "dunderheaded alarmists and prophets of doom" and "environmental wackos." On the late-night American news show "Nightline," Mr. Limbaugh, who was debating then-Senator Al Gore, said, "Mount Pinatubo has put 570 times the amount of chlorine into the atmosphere in one eruption than all the man-made chlorofluorocarbons in one year"—forgetting that chlorine and CFCs are different animals.

Although I think Mr. Limbaugh's numbers need to be carefully checked at all times, I'll just settle for simple logic. It is not given to us to control volcanoes or errant asteroids, ice ages, the arrival and departure of the atmosphere, or the frequency of big bangs. We can, and ought to, control our own excesses. I have come to like the ozone barrier. Why add to its troubles?

Mr. Limbaugh also tends to think loosely about the number of trees chopped down in our forests, about the dangers of dioxin, and about any number of other environmental concerns, long documented and accepted by scientists.

He reminds me of a less charming lad who was put out of business in the 1950s, Senator Joe McCarthy. It was not a questioning of his abuse of the facts that shamed Senator McCarthy before his formerly adoring public, but rather a simple question put to him by Joseph Welch, the attorney for the U.S. Army: "Have you no sense of decency, Sir, at long last?"

He obviously did not, and that was it. Enough was enough. "You can't fool all the people for very long."

If Mr. Limbaugh, and people like him, were to debate me, I would be tempted to repeat Welch's query or ask something like "Do you believe in compunction?" or "Are you serious?" However, as I have grown older, I have mellowed a bit. I am sometimes more curious than angry, so I would also want to ask: "How did you reach your present conclusions?" I'd listen and try to explain how I reached mine. I'd hope to persuade him that, as usual, I was right and he wasn't. And I'd try not to forget tact and resort to asking how he ever developed such a mean mouth. How did he ever come to choose Dixy Lee Ray as his expert? We have 2,000 scientists and 100 Nobel laureates who disagree with her "science." And did he ever wonder how much he and she cost the Earth?

The reason he has such a big audience is that his fans would rather feel comfortable than feel alarmed. If they feel comfortable enough, they see no reason to change their ways. But I'll bet that if you become alarmed at all the real dangers to the land, to the sources of our clean water, to the atmosphere, to the species that are disappearing, your natural inclination would probably not be to do what he does. I believe you would—and he should—think it better to get off the track before the locomotive wants your space.

You could say that the old Reagan-Bush leaguers were in it for the billions, that for all their red-white-and-blue chest pounding, they have been shills for transnational corporations. I believe Limbaugh to be sincere, but sincerely wrong.

But then there's the so-called Wise Use Movement, or as National Park Service Director Roger Kennedy calls it, "the Unwise Misuse Movement." The Wise Use mission seems to be to weaken the Endangered Species Acts, allow oil and gas development and mining in national parks and designated wilderness, and make sure anyone can travel to any part of the wilderness they want with the aid of an internal-combustion engine such as snowmobile, off-road vehicle, or dirt bike. Wise Users also have a *Me first!* idea of traditional property rights. These folks are tough. They are well funded. Fortunately, they lack grassroots members. Enough people in America understand the need for wilderness.

Here are some of the principal recent donors to the People for the West!, a Wise Use group, as reported by *Audubon* magazine:

> Nerco Minerals Co., $100,000
> Cyprus Minerals, $100,000
> Chevron USA, $45,000

Home Stake Mining Co., $15,000

Energy Fuels, $15,000

Hecla Mining Co., $30,000

Bond Gold Corp., $30,000

Pegasus Gold Corp., $15,000

I think it only natural that Chevron USA would see fit to donate $45,000 to People for the West!, since one of the organization's other missions has been to uphold the antiquated 1872 mining law governing hard-rock mining. That law let Chevron buy the 2,036 acres that make up the Stillwater mine, which sits forty miles over the Beartooth-Absaroka Wilderness from Yellowstone Park, for a total of only $10,180. That, according to the Mineral Policy Center, amounts to $5 an acre. A good deal, considering that the mine, with its reserves of palladium and platinum, is worth an estimated $30 billion.

I have nothing against making a profit. You must have accumulation from one thing in order to accomplish something else. Investments must come from somewhere. If making some money is going to encourage people to do things, fine, but I want their profit to lead them on to do good and better things. What concerns me is the impact of avarice on the Earth.

"These Wise Use extremists claim that economically you're going to take their jobs away from them; they're all going to become poor; their children are going to starve; and it's all because you're a bunch of fuzzy-headed tree huggers. . . . It's blatant lying in many cases in how they present things. . . ." This, from Gen. Norman Schwarzkopf, not usually known for his environmental radicalism. He was speaking at a press conference for the Nature Conservancy, a nongovernmental group that buys up sensitive land of notable ecological worth in order to preserve it.

Developers are entitled to just compensation when the public decides the lands they were to develop might better be put to use as, say, wilderness, rather than, say, to be clearcut for junk journals or developed into yet another ski resort. (And I have skied much of my life, as soldier and civilian.) But I do not believe a developer or timber owner should be compensated for the opportunity they may have lost. They should get what they paid out plus reasonable interest.

Otherwise, you create the opportunity for blackmailing the public. All over the West are lands left over from the checkerboard pattern of public and private ownership begun when Congress gave alternating sections to the railroads to encourage them to cross the country as quickly as possible. (Remember? They used to carry people on trains.) These parcels are sometimes in the middle of wilderness or adjoining it. Naturally, the public would like the owners not to clearcut the lands, and that desire can sometimes be manipulated, so that much more than fair market value is paid. Of course, many owners of forestlands want to do the right thing, at a fair price.

I am well aware that the Fifth Amendment to the U.S. Constitution reads, in part: "No person shall . . . be deprived of life, liberty, or property, without due process of law; nor shall private property be taken for public use without just compensation."

I believe Thomas Jefferson and James Madison had a bit of a hand in the writing of that Constitution. Here is an excerpt from a letter Jefferson wrote to Madison: "The Earth belongs in use to the living . . . no man can by natural right oblige the lands he occupies, or the persons who succeed him in that occupation, to the payment of debts contracted by him. For if he could, he might during his own life, eat up the use of the lands for several generations to come . . . then the Earth would belong to the dead and not the living generation. . . . No generation can contract debts greater than may be paid during the course of its own existence."

Wise use.

CHAPTER 22

Rule Number 6 Revisited

IT'S BEEN A WHILE since I have mentioned Rule Number 6. If you've forgotten, Rule Number 6 is: Never take yourself too seriously. This time it will be necessary to take a circuitous route to reach the rule, almost like flogging a dead horse, as you will see.

One time, Howard Zahniser, whose patience and boldness as head of The Wilderness Society were the main reasons for this country's having a wilderness system, was addressing a wilderness conference convened by the Federation of Western Outdoors Clubs, and he began his address with an account of how he, Joe Penfold, and I happened to carry a dead horse into a house in Washington, D.C.

We three were walking from Zahnie's office to dinner at the Cosmos Club. Halfway down the block from P Street to Massachusetts Avenue, we came upon the dead horse. It was not a huge workhorse, but it was not a small horse, either.

A distraught man standing beside the horse begged us to help him carry the animal up the stairs into his house, which was right there.

It was no easy task. Zahnie, whose heart condition would lead to his death just before the Wilderness Bill was signed into law by President Johnson, could not apply as much energy as he would have liked to. He portaged the horse's head end up the stairs, Joe and I the other end. You can imagine with what difficulty we pushed and shoved that dead horse into the living room. Then the man asked us to help get the horse into the bathroom and put it in the bathtub.

Once you get involved in a situation like this, it is difficult to back out. It was a tight fit, but we got the horse into the bathtub.

We finally felt that we were due at least an explanation.

"Why, for the love of the Lord, did you ask us to do this?" asked Zahnie. Of course, anyone with due intelligence would have asked the question sooner, but Zahnie put tact first.

"Well," said the man, "it's this way. I share this house with a good friend. He is out of town for the weekend, but he will be home tonight. He's a good man, and for the most part we get along well. But he is constantly doing something that at first only bothered me, but as time went by, really got to me. Almost invariably, whenever I tell him something I've learned or think might interest him, he says, 'I know.' Whatever it is, he says, 'I know,' or 'Yeah, I know.'

"So he's coming home tonight, and I'm going to be sitting in the living room reading, and because it's been a long trip, the first thing he is going to do is go to the bathroom. Then he is going to charge out of the bathroom and say: 'There's a dead horse in the bathtub!'

"And I'm going to smile and say, 'I know.'"

The only problem with this story, which I happen to like, is that not a word of it is true, save for the fact that Zahnie was tactful. He did indeed tell the story to the wilderness conference as a shaggy-dog icebreaker.

Now there is a recent book with the title *Environmental Overkill*, by Dixy Lee Ray, who was once the governor of Washington and chairman (her word) of the Atomic Energy Commission. On page 204 she ascribes this quote to me: "While the death of young men in war is unfortunate, it is no more serious than the touching of mountains and wilderness areas by humankind." This quote has many problems, but it does share one thing with Zahnie's tale: it is not true. It is made up. I lost too many good friends in World War II to have had such a comparison ever cross my mind.

In the very next paragraph, Ms. Ray recounts how I told a travel group in Whistler, British Columbia: "Loggers losing their jobs because of Spotted Owl legislation is, in my eyes, no different than people being out of work after the furnaces of Dachau shut down."

This, too, is a strong thing to say. I did not say it. Dick Cavett did—almost, but not quite.

Here's how a certain passage reads in my autobiography, *For Earth's Sake*: "How much sympathy should go to an industry that won't change its ways or workers who won't change theirs, until something has been destroyed that belongs to all the future, and not really to them?"

In environmental controversies, industry invariably brings up the question of jobs. So did Dick Cavett. When John McPhee's *Encounters with the Archdruid* was published, he asked the author to appear on his show. McPhee, with perhaps more modesty than was necessary, declined. As one might expect, the archdruid leapt at the opportunity, and was joined there by Arthur Godfrey. Mr. Cavett asked if I was alarmed by what was happening to the environment. Trying hard to sound reasonable, I gave a nondescript answer. Arthur Godfrey intervened to say, "It scares the hell out of me!"

Dick Cavett happened to look down at Mr. Godfrey's shoes, and could not forgo a comment about their being made of alligator leather. Then he went after me. "What," he asked, "do you tell those who say environmentalists are putting people out of work?"

I was about to come up with a nonconfrontational answer, but he didn't wait.

"I think I can answer that one," he said. "I suppose a lot of people lost their jobs when they closed the furnaces at Dachau."

Shocked by his own extemporaneity, he quickly changed the subject.

On the front cover of *Environmental Overkill* is a blurb from Rush Limbaugh. He says, "A way must be found to get this book into the hands of as many Americans as possible."

I wonder why?

WAIT, YOU SAY, what about Rule Number 6? Wasn't that the point? Rule Number 6 said not to take yourself so seriously. Sometimes it is hard. But you're right to insist. So I leave you with this:

Anne and I attended a party at an old friend's house not too long ago, and wandered into the kitchen. On top of the refrigerator was an unusual object. I remembered it later as an elephant's foot. She remembered it as the head of a hippopotamus. We argued about it and could not agree. We did agree that our hostess was Barbara Bedayn. To end the argument, I asked Anne to call Barbara, which she did.

"Is this Barbara?"

"Yes."

"Are you in the kitchen?"

"Yes."

"On top of the refrigerator, is that an elephant's foot or the head of a hippopotamus?"

There was a silent pause, then the answer—and all of this is true:

"Honey, I think you have the wrong number."

CHAPTER 23

Let Heaven and Nature Sing

We are compounded of dust and the light of a star.

—Loren Eiseley

THE OTHER DAY I was speaking to an audience at Grace Cathedral, the Episcopal church atop Nob Hill in San Francisco, and a very young woman asked me, "What level of hope do you allow yourself?"

I thought this was a strange question from one so young. She should have been outside. It was a sunny day, and inside she had to put up with me.

I told her I allowed very little else but hope. If I allowed myself to give up on hope, I would just have to order a Tanqueray martini—straight up, no distractions—then another and another.

She was young. She did not laugh.

Look, I said, every time you see a child come and begin to walk and learn how to talk, there it is: hope. There is this enormous capability within all of us. We keep producing it, again and again, as a species. I have hope, I said, that we will stop smothering the genius of children. What gives them a chance to blossom? *Being outdoors.* You don't get much feeling for history, for the Earth, when you spend twelve years in a concrete box trying to get educated. Under those conditions, what you become educated about are concrete boxes.

Learn to read the Earth, as Father Thomas Berry says.

A cobweb in the attic gathers dust, and is ugly. But a cobweb outdoors gathers dewdrops that scintillate in the sun. Get out. Find your hope. Read the Earth. It is an extraordinary book: full color, stereo sound, wonderful aromas, the wind. It is an extraordinary planet.

You ask me how much hope I allow myself. I get my hope when I say: Look at that living thing.

Look at mountains, also.

Notice the way rivers meander, when they need to.

I myself would like to return to the time of Moses and ask him to go back up the mountain and bring down the other tablet. The problem with the Ten Commandments is that they only talk of how we're supposed to treat each other. There's not a bloody word about how we're supposed to treat the Earth. Well, we don't and won't have each other without the Earth, and we are losing it. That other tablet must be up on the mountain still. Moses must have dropped it. Find that other tablet.

In Genesis 1:28, God tells the newly created Eve and Adam: "Be fruitful, and multiply, and replenish the earth, and subdue it:

and have dominion over the fish of the sea, and over the fowl of the air, and over every living thing that moveth upon the earth."

As Wallace Stegner put it in *Where the Bluebird Sings to the Lemonade Springs*, "Whether or not God meant it in quite that way, and whether or not men translated Him correctly, many used these words as justification to make the Earth serve human purposes alone."

John Widtsoe, a Mormon patriarch in the American West, put it most bluntly: "The destiny of man is to possess the whole Earth; the destiny of the Earth is to be subject to man. There can be no full conquest of the Earth, and no real satisfaction to humanity, if large portions of the Earth remain beyond his highest control."

In another essay, Stegner commented upon Widtsoe's witlessness: "That doctrine offends me to the bottom of my not-very-Christian soul."

I agree.

Stegner was zeroing in on that word "subdue." Some scholarly friends of mine maintain that the original meaning was "steward" the Earth. Think of the difference a one-word injunction makes, over 2,000 years. For the future, let's try "protect."

Genesis was probably written when the population of the Earth was 50 million. Jesus Christ was born when the population was about 200 million. It is quite a different ball game, these days, when the population is 6 billion, and we're using up those fish and their seas, those fowl and the air they fly through, and every living thing—including the cattle and the soil and streamsides they trample.

Isaiah had the right idea, if we are interpreting him properly, when he said: "Woe unto them that join house to house, that lay field to field, till there be no place, that they may be placed alone in the midst of the earth!"

To me, God and Nature are synonymous, and neither could wait the billions of years before man arrived to decide what to look like. I hear that two scientists were discussing the big bang, and God, leaning over their shoulders, asked, "Which big bang?" I have as much trouble comprehending Creation as I do comprehending what it was created out of. I like mystery, the unending search for truth, the truth of beauty. I would have no use for pearly gates and streets of gold if canyon wrens were not admitted.

CHAPTER 24

For Those Who Would Save the Earth

Whatever you can do, or dream you can, begin it.
Boldness has genius, power and magic in it.

— Johann Wolfgang von Goethe

IN *The Scottish Himalayan Expedition*, mountaineer William H. Murray reflected on the organization and will-power necessary to begin the expedition:

Until one is committed there is hesitancy, the chance to draw back, always ineffectiveness. Concerning all acts of initiative (and creation), there is one elementary truth, the ignorance of which kills countless ideas and splendid plans: that the moment one definitely commits oneself, then Providence moves, too. All sorts of things occur to help one that would never otherwise have occurred. A whole stream of events issues from the decision, raising in one's favour all manner of unforeseen incidents and meetings and material assistance, which no man could have dreamt would have come his way.

In the not-so-distant past, I saw Murray's remark on commitment serve almost as religion for the people, including me, who helped keep dams out of Dinosaur National Monument, the Yukon, and the Grand Canyon, who helped keep loggers with itchy axes out of Olympic National Park; who helped ban DDT; who helped establish the National Wilderness Preservation System and additions to the National Park System in the North Cascades, Kings Canyon, the Redwoods, Great Basin, at Point Reyes, the Golden Gate, Cape Cod, Fire Island.

We helped do all this with a Sierra Club membership less than one-tenth of its present size. Even our success in gaining passage of the Alaska National Interest Lands Conservation Act of 1980 was accomplished with a far smaller club than now exists.

Back then the Sierra Club made all this possible by boldly asserting itself. It took the words of John Muir to heart: "Climb the mountains and get their good tidings."

There are now millions of dues-paying environmentalists in the United States alone. Some count the number at 10 million. There are more; they just haven't signed up yet. But whatever the number, they don't seem to have anywhere near the power they should.

What are the reasons for this? The quick and dirty answer is: lack of boldness, smug leadership, battles over turf, absence from the legislative arena, bureaucracy, and no fun.

LET'S START by talking about Benton MacKaye's Theory of How to Build Big by Starting Small. Benton MacKaye was the father—the conceptualizer—of the Appalachian Trail. He was the first person, that I know of, to conceive of an organized wilderness system. He liked to come south to Washington, D.C., to escape the rigors of a Boston winter, and he would stay at the Cosmos Club, which had been started by John Wesley Powell with an eye toward bringing science to the attention of Congress. Benton was in his eighties when we began our chats, and he had another decade of wisdom ahead of him.

"If you want an organization of cannibals," Benton would say, "then only cannibals may be admitted." He would pause while you took in the import of that remark. Here's what he meant:

In the beginning get only the people who think the way you do, who believe. Put your act together with them, and make the idea and the organization as strong as you can, before you launch it to the public. This is the way to build an organization with real power.

Make it very clear what the organization stands for. Let that be known, and let that be the welcome mat for anyone who wants to come under your tent.

If you start worrying from the outset about pleasing too much or offending certain people or certain groups, then you're already lost. You've got to let people know you are not going to sell out, that you are not going to waffle on the basic principles. You can say, "I haven't reached all my conclusions yet; I may not be all that practical. But this is the way I think it ought to be, and we stand for that." Then see who joins and what happens.

On the other hand, I don't believe in purity. That's another mistake. It is ironic, but being too pure is about the same as being too practical. Practical people have made all their decisions, as I said a bit earlier. They have lost the ability to listen, and are determined to repeat the errors of their ancestors. Purists are just practical people who have gone even further than necessary.

Once the organization is off the ground, don't be so quick to take credit for every victory. That's the time to work on coalition building. Howard Zahniser didn't seek to have The Wilderness Society take credit for everything, even when it could have. Again and again he would say, They did it, those other people. He gave other groups the credit. The idea is not to claim turf. The idea is to save turf. How do we build a constituency for the Earth?

If your purism consists of love for life and for the only planet we know to have life on it, I'll accept that. But don't then say you've got to love it in the following manner, and by the numbers. Love it your own way, and if you have a better way, please tell me about it.

The modern environmental movement seems to be having trouble with leadership. Who are the leaders? Where is the charisma? Environmental groups go to Hollywood to find a sympathetic celebrity to provide them with glitz. Where are our own charismatic leaders, whom the media would want to quote directly?

I learned a lot about leadership on the early Sierra Club High Trips. These trips were set up by John Muir and attorney Will Colby to get people into the wilderness where they could have fun and fall in love with the wild. It was a simple strategy. They did fall in love with the mountains, and many of these people went on to lead corporations, become artists and writers, and move in political circles. They never forgot the wilderness.

There were mules and camp fires on the High Trips, lots of stories and laughter, sometimes up to two hundred people on the same four-week outing. I was the leader in 1939–1941 and again in 1946–1956. You had to be the benign dictator. If you asked everybody individually where they wanted to camp the next day, you'd have chaos. Perhaps the leaders could have taken a different trail or climbed toward a different pass, but this would have had to be determined earlier, when the logistics were worked out.

We were open at the planning stage, but once we got started, we would say: Have a good time, take all the detours you want, walk with your own friends. You don't have to go in lockstep. But here is where we are camping at the end of the day, at the foot of Tilden Lake, or wherever, because that's where the supplies will be, and dinner.

We couldn't have people all over the mountain. It would have been unsafe and increased the trip's impact on the mountain.

One of the reasons certain groups don't work too well, as of yet, is that they are so busy looking for consensus and fighting hierarchy that they miss the forests *and* the trees. Too much consensus makes it too easy for the lowest common denominator to rule. The group is not going to get "felled in."

That's what Cpl. Wid Corn used to say when I was in the Tenth Mountain Division. "Come on, you guys, quit melling around and get felled in."

That is what's happening with the Green Party. They are melling around and not getting felled in. They argue. They argue some more. They agonize about hierarchy. They don't want to offend anyone. But they disdain having character. They don't seem to want to let anybody lead, and leaders are necessary.

How far can you extend this concept? Not too far. The danger comes when someone tries to say: This is the way it is, and I'm the leader, and I am going to continue to be the leader, and don't anybody get in my way. It is very important that leadership change.

Once in a while (a great while) I'm grateful the Sierra Club didn't want me to be its executive director forever. That was a good thing for all hands, although I didn't feel so good about it at the time.

I like to pose this question: What do environmentalists, feminists, the far-righteous, the right-to-lifers, and the Bible have in common? Answer: No humor. No one has disagreed yet.

Of course, maybe we need two Green Parties, the light green and the dark green. That is, Republican and Democrat, conservative and progressive. The environmental movement needs to be much more a part of political discussion in this country. This was the reason I founded the League of Conservation Voters, so that we could see who was voting on the side of the Earth, and who was out there trashing it.

By whatever means, we need to send a message: It would be nice to make a new try at practicing democracy.

HOW DO YOU bring politicians onto the side of saving the Earth?

The first thing you do is show them what they are saving, as we did on those High Trips, or as John Muir did when he camped in Yosemite with President Theodore Roosevelt. Roosevelt went away rhapsodizing about natural cathedrals. Back in Washington, he helped to protect a great deal of wilderness from those in his own party who wanted to scalp, pulp, and package everything that lay between the cities. They did a pretty good job of that in Michigan, Wisconsin, Oregon, and Washington, in Roosevelt's time. At the rim of the Grand Canyon, he could say, "Leave it as it is. The ages have been at work on it, and man can only mar it."

Roosevelt didn't need much convincing. At a time when he was severely depressed, after his wife and daughter had tragically and suddenly died, he came to the Badlands of the Dakotas and Montana with the idea of healing himself in wildness. When he left that open prairie life and returned to politics, he knew what had saved him, and he knew it was what could save the country, and all of us.

Representative John Saylor of Pennsylvania started out as a conservative Republican, too. America's wild rivers, rather than our wild prairie, influenced him. Many politicians yearn to have structures built in their names, but John Saylor didn't build a monument. He saved one: Dinosaur National Monument.

In the early 1950s the Bureau of Reclamation and its water-greedy supporters, who wanted the Echo Park and Split Mountain dams built in the Upper Colorado Basin, put out that anyone who considered rafting the Yampa or Green rivers must possess a severe death wish. This was in the days before millions of young Americans reclaimed our wilderness with rafts, kayaks, horses, llamas, and high-tech shoes.

John Saylor decided to go out and look at what he would be voting to flood (or cut)—something not enough senators and members of Congress are willing to do. He brought along his son, and also Joseph W. Penfold, who was the solemnly humorous Western leader of the Izaak Walton League. Penfold brought his son, too. It was Joe who once said, "The engineers in the Bureau of Reclamation are like beavers. They can't stand the sight of running water." Joe, John, and the two sons got their feet wet on the Yampa, and that's not all. Saylor returned to Congress a bull-dog for wilderness.

When we were being badgered by the House Committee on Interior and Insular Affairs, a group of gentlemen who could never understand how anything could ever take precedence over the orderly eradication of wilderness, John would save us. His voice would rise, stentorian vibrations rumbled, his usually amused countenance turned stern, and soon he was plucking information from commissioners, secretaries, and agency technicians that the bureaucrats did not want out. John Saylor learned to spot rapids on the Green. When he got back to Washington, he spotted truth-substitutes, which is what antienvironmental bureaucrats used to like to spread before they spread disinformation.

There are bureaucrats in the environmental movement, too. The cure for them is the same as it is for politicians: Get out of Washington (or San Francisco, New York, Los Angeles) and listen to the mountains. Float the rivers. It is too easy to lose touch with the grass, with the grass roots. Don't ever give up what you haven't seen.

And don't be unwilling to make yourself a little unpopular by trying to protect something that people want to unprotect.

Some environmentalists will do anything to preserve their access, imagined or real, to power.

I once had an illuminating conversation with John Baker, who was then president of the National Audubon Society. John Baker told me that Harold Ickes, who was Franklin Roosevelt's Secretary of the Interior and one of the greatest, had complained to him that he was "having some trouble with your Audubon ladies in the Southeast." They were concerned about threats to the ivory-billed woodpecker. Baker told the "Audubon ladies" to go easy, which they did.

"After that," John told me, "I never had trouble getting an appointment with Harold Ickes."

But the ivory-billed woodpecker is extinct.

Access to power is good. It makes things easier when a Bob Marshall is running the recreation division of the Forest Service or a Hazel O'Leary is Secretary of Energy instead of a Dixy Lee Ray. But when access is not there, as it rarely was during the Reagan administration, we still have our recourse: boycotts, voting, the truth, the courts, and the strong desire of most Americans to drink clean water, to have their children breathe clean air, and to have their grandchildren experience what it means to be able to walk beyond the roads.

You can never tell when a slight push in the right direction will move politicians who want to be moved or who make up their own minds from time to time. President Jimmy Carter had a dozen of us in the White House to explain, among other things, why he could not veto legislation authorizing the Clinch River Breeder Reactor—bad nuclear news. Before departing, I handed him a letter signed by me but written by Jeff Knight, Friends of the Earth's energy expert in Washington. In one page plus four lines, Jeff explained why the president should veto the bill and what the consequences would be.

Having already explained why he couldn't, Jimmy Carter did.

Moral 1: Write a good letter—and hand-carry it!

Moral 2: Thank your benefactor.

I met again with Jimmy Carter, when he was no longer president. It was the day the reactivated Tenth Mountain Division, my old outfit, arrived peacefully on Haiti. Were it not for Carter's intervention the day before, many Americans and Haitians would already have been dead and many more about to be.

By the simple expedient of trying to be fair, Carter got the U.S. out of a rut, just as he had a few months earlier in North Korea. Carter is a president, wrongly abused by the media, who has managed to recreate himself in a short space of time. I was reminded that war is the ultimate environmental disaster and that Carter had managed to avert disaster twice in one year. I smiled at the irony that so many pundits, ever ready to heap abuse on President Clinton at the sight of the first body bag bringing a Tenth Mountain man home, would be furious at President Carter for denying them that opportunity. I guess peace is simply too dull for some members of the media to endure.

Part of the problem, too, is that the haves of the world are still treating the have-nots as the colonies of old were treated, and this has a bad effect upon what irreplaceable wilderness we have left. The haves lend money to the erstwhile colonies, insisting that most of what they lend be spent at the source, in the donor country. To pay back the loan, the have-nots invest in cash crops for the haves, produced most abundantly on their best land. That forces them into the poorer soil of their wildlands in order to produce food for their own subsistence. Where rain forests exist, they become early victims. The forests are logged for cash, then replaced by cattle, also sold for cash, and also maintaining high cholesterol levels in their high-living customers.

Thus, the haves are destroying wilderness by ricochet.

In 1994, at a meeting of the Canadian Environmental Network (a network of some 1,800 organizations) in Ottawa, Brian Staszenski and I launched the idea of forming the Ecological Council of the Americas. There isn't anything modest about the name, but then a certain amount of boldness is required to counteract what we see wrong with NAFTA, the North America Free Trade Agreement. What we see wrong is the implication that there must be no environmental barriers to North American trade. What we see right is that there must be no trade barriers to achieving a sustainable environment, without which there can be no trade at all.

We forget that we are all in this together, the haves and the have-nots.

I once asked William Reilly, appointed by President Bush to direct the Environmental Protection Agency, what the flowers-to-brickbats ratio was during his term. He answered by quoting his predecessor, William Ruckelshaus: "The day you come and the day you leave, you get flowers. All the rest of the time it rains."

Randy Hayes, of the Rainforest Action Network, thinks environmentalists can sometimes be overly preoccupied with access because so many lawyers came into the movement in the

1980s. Lawyers are by nature negotiators, and this, thinks Randy, led to some trade-offs with things like the North American Free Trade Agreement and with GATT (General Agreement on Tariffs and Trade).

I have great respect for lawyers, however, so long as they've all gone through some sort of therapy.

Lawyers elect to be schizo. They choose to represent a John Muir on one case and a Rush Limbaugh on another. They are like the man who said, "I'm trying to follow the teachings of Jesus Christ and Mephistopheles, and I'm having problems."

In the late 1940s a lawyer told me, "Nature has no rights." He was wrong. More recent lawyers now allow the Earth its rights.

Lawyers stopped the Storm King pumped-storage hydropower scheme on the Hudson River. Lawsuits stopped the dewatering of Mono Lake by the City of Los Angeles. They have begun the process of saving the ancient forests of the Northwest by showing a federal judge, a staunch Reagan appointee, how federal agencies like the Forest Service have engaged in a pattern of lawlessness in willfully giving away, at a fraction of its value, the public treasure to timber companies, and endangering the Endangered Species Acts in regard to the spotted owl. Lawyers have become invaluable. I like a full arsenal.

OF COURSE, I never wanted a level playing field. I'm a mountaineer.

I don't always like to win. Some lessons are better learned the other way. Losing can demonstrate the need for reform—and a new way of achieving it. The way you learn not to touch a hot stove is by touching it.

Many environmental organizations are not operating on a level playing field because their tax-deductible status prevents their lobbying vigorously enough and forbids their being political. The Sierra Club does not have this problem since, as one of my finer acts, I lost the club its tax-deductible status in the Grand Canyon battle.

We saved the Grand Canyon. Who gives a damn whether your yearly dues are deductible? Nobody. By not being deductible, the organization can support direct political activity.

I have been preaching for a long time that deductible environmental organizations need a separate corporation that functions as a nondeductible associate. Decisions are made by an independent board, funds are never commingled, but there is a continuity of mission, and there can be enough overlap of directors, under current tax law, to make that independence and continuity possible.

I should add that I got the tax-deductible Sierra Club Foundation under way six years before the IRS attacked the club. This attack produced a big surge in club membership, in the same way that James Watt's flop as secretary of the interior under President Reagan brought as many as a million new recruits to the environmental cause.

The head of one effective environmental organization separates those who would like to join the movement to save the Earth, but who are doing nothing, into three groups: those who need direction, those who need motivation, and those who have just plain given up. So many people want to help if only given a chance.

Look at MBAs, whom many might consider a hard choice for environmental recruitment. But MBAs need to learn what their talents are for. What they are learning is how to cash in faster. That's not even for the birds. They should be learning what it costs to fail to lead us into a sustainable society.

We've got great things to do. Life is a school of opportunities. (Don't call them problems.) Some people just need to become excited. They need to learn that they can change things.

I get these letters from old people's organizations that are concerned about entitlements: "You made these investments. Now you deserve all the stuff back." I want my age-mates— those who are not dead—to think about something else besides their entitlements. What have they cost the Earth, during their time on it? What can they pay *back* now? Not with a lot of money, but with their energy buttressed by the wisdom they have accumulated. This is another opportunity for them. It'll make them a lot happier to think about fixing up the Earth than it will to ruminate upon their ailments.

In our society old people are put out to pasture. I don't believe in pasteurized elders. I would remind them that Theodore Roosevelt said, "It is better to wear out than to rust out."

The trick is to move my contemporaries around and aim them in the right direction.

Wallace Stegner used to say, "Walk softly and break no twigs." That may have been what he thought he was best at. Myself, I've always been a twig breaker. If the twigs are breaking and you hear the sound, you wake up to the fact that there's an opportunity. You try to work out a deal with reasonable people who aren't breaking twigs. Walking in bear country, it's better to break twigs than to surprise a bear because you didn't.

I once ran a piece of Stegner's called the "The Battle Between the Cowboys and the Bird Watchers" in the *Sierra Club Bulletin*. *Harper's* magazine had not accepted it. At the end, Stegner quoted Senator Arthur Watkins of Utah, who asked: "Why don't you have wilderness near the cities where more people can use it?" Stegner answered, "It was not given to man to create wilderness, but he can create deserts, and has."

Stegner, long a Sierra Club friend, wrote a devastating letter in the fracas that led to my walking the plank as executive director. He accused me of having been "bitten by the worm of power." More people remember that than his apology. So I say to the heads of environmental organizations: If you are going to get into fights, avoid people who happen to be extraordinarily articulate. They say strong things they may not quite mean just because that's the way they say anything. If you have to get into a fight with a master, make sure he or she stutters.

When Stegner's piece was typeset, I needed to shorten a few lines for the printer by getting rid of the widows and orphans, dangling words at the tops and bottoms of columns. You couldn't do that to Stegner's copy. There was inevitability in what he'd written. You couldn't add a word or take a word away. It was right. I began to wonder, how the hell did they get rid of the orphans and widows in the Bible?

We've lost some of those literary champions of wilderness and the environment. When you have photographers like Ansel Adams and Eliot Porter, and writers like Wallace Stegner, Loren Eiseley, Nancy Newhall, and Rachel Carson appearing in an organization's magazine and publishing books under the environmental banner, the high ground is easily captured. Those special books won many of our battles for us, sitting there on the coffee tables until people of great power looked into them and began to understand. Truth and beauty can still win battles. We need more art, more passion, more wit in defense of the Earth.

I THINK the real reason I was fired in 1969 after seventeen years as executive director of the Sierra Club was my opposition to developing nuclear power at Diablo Canyon in California. Until that moment, my other faults, which were beyond number, were tolerated, even forgiven. Then suddenly I was like Clark Kerr, president of the University of California from 1958 to 1967, who said, "I came to my job the same way I left it—fired with enthusiasm."

You must have an instinct for the future, if you are to lead environmental organizations. Nuclear power is not in the best interests of the future of this planet. Alan Watts once told me, "A star is a planet on which intelligent beings experimented with atomic power." Last year, architect William McDonough told a group of us, "In the last few decades, the U.S. has spent half a trillion dollars subsidizing something nobody wants—radioactivity."

At times you need to take some risks to save the future. Pacific Gas & Electric must regret it took the risk I warned against—the threat to the future. The power company blithely told its rate-payers that the Diablo Canyon nuclear reactors would cost less than $400 million. So far, PG&E has spent $5 billion and counting, and decommissioning looms ahead, as an added, unknown, potentially disastrous expense.

Taking risks has been my trouble in the environmental movement. Because I was a climber, I am aware that there's a certain amount of danger in getting off level ground. When you get up to where the holds are very thin and there's a great deal of air under your feet, you know that it's not a good time to slip because you might not survive it. Perhaps that is why I have always liked this quotation: "A ship in harbor is safe, but that's not what ships were built for." I like to get out of port. I think we were built to explore.

I have my regrets. I regret having hurt people. In the thick of things, you can become abrasive. Once a friend was working me over on budgetary matters, or I thought he was. He said, "I'm only trying to protect you." I reacted angrily, and said, "You protect me with the back of your hand."

I hurt him, and had not meant to. That flip statement did not come from an educated heart. An uneducated heart makes many mistakes. Better to change minds than create grudges.

Don't forget Rule Number 6. And have a good time saving the world, or you're just going to depress yourself.

People want to be part of something fun. It's exciting to change the world. If you're in it simply out of worry or guilt, you won't last, and normal people won't join you. People want to love life, if love hasn't been crushed out of them when they were children. Learning to read the Earth and saving it is fascinating stuff. Put fun in the movement to conserve, preserve, and restore, and celebrate it, and people will run to sign up.

Otherwise, once again, it can only be Tanqueray time (it's about time I got a grant from Tanqueray), and time to drink deep of despondency. But as Lord Snow said, "Despair is a sin."

I've had some big ideas in my life. I've made some things happen. I've stopped some misguided people from trashing the Earth. But the idea I believe I will be checking out on is restoration, although I have no intention of checking out any sooner than necessary. I've grown very fond of this planet. I want to help save a taste of paradise for our children. Give us back Hetch Hetchy and Glen Canyon, and I'll go quietly.

I JOURNEYED to the Himalayas when I was sixty-four. As I made the approach to Mount Everest, I thought back to William Murray: "The moment one definitely commits oneself, then Providence moves, too."

Perhaps at this moment in our time on Earth, we should all drop back about 200 years and consider again this couplet from Johann Wolfgang von Goethe:

Whatever you can do, or dream you can, begin it.
Boldness has genius, power and magic in it.

Do you have magic in you? You bet. Magic is that little genetic genius that has been evolving for three billion years: It connects us all to each other and to everything that has come before and that still lives on the planet. That is some magic, and it was formed in wilderness.

Let us begin. Let us restore the Earth. Let the mountains talk, and the rivers run.

Once more, and forever.

Afterword

IT WOULD BE EASY to talk about how much has changed since Steve and I put together the first version of this book for Earth Day 1995, but I would much rather talk about how much has changed since the 1999 Seattle meeting of the World Trade Organization (WTO). I was in Seattle (thanks to my manager Mikhail Davis) and poet Robert Arthur Lewis was there at least long enough to pass out 300 copies of a poem that describes why we came so well that, I confess, to say more would be superfluous, but that has never stopped me from saying more anyway.

Robert's poem moved me when I first read it, moves me still, and I hope it moves you now.

Why We Are Here
for the World Trade Organization Ministerial Summit, Seattle 1999

Because the world we had imagined, the one
we had always counted on
is disappearing.
Because the sun has become cancerous
and the planet is getting hotter.
Because children are starving in the shadows
of yachts and economic summits.
Because there are already too many planes in the sky.

This is the manufactured world
you have come here to codify and expedite.
We have come to tell you
there is something else we want to buy.

What we want, money no longer recognizes
like the vitality of nature, the integrity of work.
We don't want cheaper wood, we want living trees.
We don't want engineered fruit, we want to see and smell the
food growing
in our own neighborhoods.

We are here because a voice inside us,
a memory in our blood, tells us
you are not just a trade body, you are the blind tip
of a dark wave which has forgotten its source.
We are here to defend and honor
what is real, natural, human and basic
against this rising tide of greed.

We are here by the insistence of spirit and by the authority of
nature.
If you doubt for one minute the power of truth
or the primacy of nature
try not breathing for that length of time.

Now you know the pressure of our desire.
We are not here to tinker with your laws.
We are here to change you from the inside out.
This is not a political protest.
It is an uprising of the soul.

—*Robert Arthur Lewis*

The day of November 30, 1999 began like so many thousands of others, waking up early in the house I have occupied since 1947 in Berkeley with my wife, Anne, who has occupied me for three years longer than that. But by 9 AM, I stood watching history unfold under a soft rain in Seattle's Denny Park. Tom Hayden was speaking to a crowd of about 1,000 Sierra Club members and others who understood what the WTO and the corporations it serves are doing to the Earth. Tom Hayden, who has lost little of his fire despite his transition from the Chicago Seven to the California Senate, reminded us that people have always had to take to the streets to get the moneyed interests to listen. And did the crowd ever take to the streets. Over 50,000 people marched on, blockaded, or otherwise demonstrated at the WTO meeting that day. Hundreds were arrested, thousands (demonstrators and otherwise) were pepper-sprayed, tear-gassed, shot with rubber bullets, or beaten by police before the week of meetings ended. But when it was announced on Friday, December 3, 1999 that the meetings had failed completely and no new powers had been granted to the WTO by its member countries, people around the world rejoiced. But why?

As I quipped to Mikhail Gorbachev several years ago, "We're watching Russia very closely, and if you can make Democracy work, we're gonna try it." He laughed, and most people do, but isn't it sad that it's funny? We don't have Democracy in this country. What we have is legal bribery, where politicians must raise so much money to get elected that by the time they do, they're bought and paid for by the companies and wealthy individuals who financed their campaigns. While most major campaign contributors support "free" trade policies, most Americans have grave reservations. It is no surprise whose position has prevailed throughout the 1990s.

While the usual half of American voters declined to vote at all, the transnational corporations, with help from their friends in Washington, DC, got the rules of the global economy rewritten to protect corporate profits at the expense of everything else. In Seattle, Americans finally woke up, and perhaps just in time.

A full-page ad that ran the week of the World Trade Organization Ministerial meeting read: "When the state becomes the servant of corporations it's called fascism. When the corporations create their own super-state, it's called the WTO." The general WTO idea is to keep the environment, human rights, workers' rights, and peace from getting in the way of world trade. Member countries (over 100, including the U.S.) can be required to change food safety, environmental protection, labor, and any other kind of national or local law that could be construed by another country to be a barrier to trade. Rulings on what constitutes a "barrier" are made in secret by three member panels of trade lawyers who know nothing about the Earth and its unique species and cultures. I like kangaroos quite well, having visited them in Australia. I have no such fondness for kangaroo courts like the WTO.

The WTO is ten for ten on the environment so far. Ten WTO challenges to national environmental protection laws, ten laws weakened. This includes such hallowed legislation as the Clean Air Act, the Endangered Species Act, and the Marine Mammal Protection Act. After Sam LaBudde and others worked so hard to get protection for dolphins who were netted and killed by tuna fisherman, the Clinton Administration folded under the pressure of a trade-court ruling and weakened the Dolphin-Safe label to allow Mexican and Venezuelan tuna fisherman to encircle and harass dolphins just like the old days, just so long as no one actually "sees" a dolphin killed. Few people had ever seen a dolphin killed by tuna fishing until Sam risked his life to expose it, but they were dying by the tens of thousands just the same. And soon may be again, thanks to "free" trade.

Citizens whose governments got involved in the North American Free-Trade Agreement (NAFTA) have even fewer rights to protect their environment, their health, or their jobs. Under "investment" and "intellectual property" provisions that NAFTA fans were trying to put into the WTO, a corporation of another country can actually sue a government for damages if it even tries to pass a law to protect public health that also happens to hurt their profits. The Canadian Parliament merely discussed banning a toxic gas additive and had to shell out millions of dollars to the US-based producer of the stuff, apparently for having hurt their corporate image. I hope you can see where this is all going.

Or *was* going. In Seattle, Ralph Nader's chief trade expert Lori Wallach put it best: "the unstoppable force called economic globalization just hit the immovable object called grassroots democracy."

Grassroots democracy had received a shot in the arm the previous March, at the always impressive Land, Air, and Water Conference in Eugene, Oregon, when a few locked-out members of the United Steelworkers of America (USWA) and some enviros got a meeting going in the bar that I'll always remember. We shared regret over what corporate raider Charles Hurwitz was doing to our redwoods, working people, and our economies, if not his own. We declared an alliance and soon cemented it in Eureka, California. I was delighted to be invited to co-chair the coalition with USWA's David Foster, who later described our mission so beautifully that it must be repeated as often as possible:

If you will promise to make sustainable jobs
a product of environmental protection,
we will promise to make environmental protection
our most important job.

To which I added, feebly by comparison:

We promise that the Alliance will be the conscience
for corporations, investors, and politicians who have lost theirs.
They want to keep us tied up in a jobs-versus-the-environment contest.
The real imperative is to create a world where we all have jobs-for-the-
environment.

The transnational corporations and big investors are suffering from a strain of potentially fatal short-sightedness I call *Ecomyopia*. If the symptoms include a complete loss of the ability to foresee consequences, what's the cure? Start by realizing there *are* limits to Growth. Then ask:

What kinds of Growth must we have?
What kinds can we no longer afford?

Restorative businesses that can help make the economy safe for Life on Earth, employee-owned companies that promote economic equity and long-term planning, these are just a few examples of some kinds of economic growth that would do us some good. The economic growth of the WTO, where the rich get richer and our children inherit a toxic, threadbare planet, is something not even Bill Gates can afford.

My friend Nancy Newhall once called for us to live on the Earth in such a way that no creature "snake nor butterfly, be hindered from its errand." But what is our own errand? Perhaps we have forgotten, and must remember that every species alive has an errand: to share, restore, and celebrate the Earth. From other species we can re-learn commerce; the cycles of Nature restore everything. And *nothing* is wasted. Everything is made ready for the next use and next user. You wouldn't ask a bee to opt for a job *or* the environment. In the course of doing its "job" of gathering food to insure the survival of its hive, it pollinates the wild plants and domestic crops that make the world livable (and edible!) for the rest of us. If our cleverness with chemicals and genes kills off bees and other crop pollinators, even Wall Street would notice (and they generally only care about one kind of green ... Greenspan!). Perhaps we could get their attention if we revoked the right of Federal Reserve Chairman Greenspan to use the word "green" in his name, until he does the arithmetic on what his mastery of economic growth is costing the Earth and the future.

As we look to the future, we can say, "Remember Seattle!" Remember the tens of thousands of people, students, Steelworkers, and Earth First!ers alike, who took to the streets to take back democracy. Remember "free" trade champion President Clinton disappointing his corporate allies by publicly conceding that protecting workers and the environment must become part of the WTO's mandate. Well said, as always, but not, I fear, well believed by the speaker or his vice-president.

Remember how the police became unwitting handmaidens of the transnational corporations. For this World War II veteran, the ruthless efficiency of the Seattle police evoked memories of German soldiers who followed orders instead of thinking. They were too young to understand whose interests their brutal actions served. I don't have the problem of being too young any more, so I watched the police riot from the safety of my motel room television set.

Among those pepper-sprayed was author and former-CEO Paul Hawken, who recently released the authoritative book on corporations that are doing well financially by doing good for the Earth (*Natural Capitalism*, with Amory and Hunter Lovins: read it). Paul took to the streets of Seattle to confront the dark side of the corporate world, which refuses to respect anything but profit and endless growth. In his stirring account of November 30, 1999, N30, Paul writes that the people who filled the streets represented "everything the WTO left behind." I was proud to hear that this included 40 representatives of Friends of the Earth International from 20 countries. It also included thousands of young people who didn't want to inherit the faster, simpler world offered by the WTO. I have been here for almost nine decades now and I like the planet in all its confusing richness of cultures and creatures. I wouldn't want anything less for my grandchildren.

We can no longer afford the luxury of pessimism and, after Seattle, it is entirely unnecessary. The group we had formed with the Steelworkers, the Alliance for Sustainable Jobs and the Environment, was not deterred but immeasurably strengthened by the struggle. Other large unions we marched with in Seattle are ready to join up. We should all congratulate each other on winning the first round in Seattle, but the future depends on how we follow through. The WTO is reeling and the opportunity in *Natural Capitalism* for corporations to do the right thing is clearer than ever. Earth still hangs in the balance, but right now the scales are beginning to tip our way for the first time in decades. Won't you join the party? Who says saving the world can't be fun?

Faith on the Line

Faith on the Line

Charles Colson

VICTOR BOOKS

A DIVISION OF SCRIPTURE PRESS PUBLICATIONS INC.
USA CANADA ENGLAND

Editor: Barbara Williams
Cover Design: Scott Rattray

Unless otherwise indicated, Scripture references are from the
New American Standard Bible, © the Lockman Foundation,
1960, 1962, 1963, 1968, 1971, 1972, 1973, 1977; other references are
from the *Holy Bible, New International Version* ® (NIV).
Copyright © 1973, 1978, 1984 by International Bible Society.
Used by permission of Zondervan Publishing House. All rights reserved; and the *Authorized (King James) Version* (KJV).

Library of Congress Cataloging-in-Publication Data

Colson, Charles W.
  Faith on the line / by Charles Colson.
    p.   cm.
  This book has been expanded from the "Challenging the church"
series, published by Victor Books, 1986 — T. p. verso.
  ISBN 1-56476-131-2
  1. Church renewal — United States. 2. United States — Moral conditions. 3. Church and social problems — United States. 4. Witness
bearing (Christianity) 5. Evangelistic work — United States.
6. Church and the world. 7. United States — Church history — 20th
century. I. Colson, Charles W. Challenging the church. II. Title.
BR526.C63   1993
261'.1'0973 — dc20   93-19217
                                                                                    CIP

2   3   4   5   6   7   8   9   10   Printing/Year   98   97   96   95   94

CONTENTS

PUBLISHER'S NOTE

Chuck Colson's prophetic call
to the church and her people is
by no means new. Much of this material
appeared in his earlier four-book
"Challenging the Church" series
published by Victor Books.

Believing the timeliness and
timelessness of Chuck's message,
we now offer this updated,
one-volume edition, with the hope that you
will be freshly challenged
to put your faith on the line.

INTRODUCTION

Faith on the Line was previously published as a series of small books taken from speeches I delivered in the early 1980s, in which I called Christians to a righteous, holy life unconformed to the culture. Looking back, evangelicals were living in relative ease. A few years earlier, *Newsweek* had declared "the year of the evangelical."

But in the mid-1980s came scandals involving several prominent evangelical leaders. In the 1988 presidential election the public viewed evangelicals and the religious right as just another special interest group. And as the 1990s dawned, a Gallup poll found that evangelicals are among the most feared people in America.

Today, a "culture war" rages in our nation: the struggle between two conflicting worldviews. On one side are those who cleave to a Judeo-Christian understanding of absolute truth, with a corresponding view of life and culture based on two central commandments—love for God and love for people. On the other side are those who believe truth can be defined by each individual, with a corresponding view of life and culture based on individual choice—"what's right for me."

The culture war escalates with each passing day, as those two diametrically opposed perspectives face off on issues like abortion, the militant homosexual agenda, the cause and cure for crime, medical ethics, education, and economics.

Never before has the need been more urgent for Christians to bring their faith to the front lines. Christians must be equipped to articulate a Christian apologetic on the issues. It takes courage to think and act Christianly in times like these.

But in any age Christians are called to declare the truth through holy living and an unashamed declaration of the truth. We must demonstrate Christian love and compassion to even those who oppose us most vehemently. And so the message of those speeches I delivered a decade ago is as relevant as ever, even though in some places it was updated to fit today's cultural context.

If you're familiar with my other books, this one will serve as a refreshing reminder of familiar themes; if you're new to my writing, this book will be a good introduction. In either case, as you read the pages that follow, I pray God will use them for His purposes in your life—and that you might put your faith on the line each day, for His glory in the course of the battle for the hearts and minds of our culture.

Charles W. Colson
August 11, 1993

CHAPTER ONE

Dare to Be Different, Dare to Be Christian

Amerca is a nation in transition, in the eye of a storm that pollster Daniel Yankelovich has called a "sweeping, irreversible cultural revolution . . . transforming the rules that once guided American life." Powerful forces are shaking our very substructure.

Like all revolutions, the most profound struggle is going on in *us*. We are desperately seeking certainty in the midst of confusion and hope in the face of disillusionment. Above all, we are confounded by the maddening contradictions that plague us. Consider these few illustrations:

● The boundless affluence considered to be the fulfillment of the American dream led to indifference and spiritually destructive materialism.

● The technology that promised to lead us to a new promised land now threatens to poison it—a toxic no man's land.

● The self-fulfillment spree of the past decades led not to the expected expansion of the human potential but to isolation, loneliness, and the death of community.

Our dilemmas are compounded by a technology that dramatically telescopes history, accelerating the speed of cultural change. While it took early pioneers a full century on foot and hoof to hack their way across the wilderness of this continent, the jet age measures such distance in hours and seconds. So today's pilgrimage is that of a people being propelled through a wind tunnel, tumbling and falling helplessly, unable to gain secure footing long enough to catch their breath.

Jacques Ellul, the French lawyer-theologian, wrote:

Day after day the wind blows away the
pages of our calendars, our newspapers,
and our political regimes, and we glide
along the stream of time without a
judgment.... If we are able to live in this
world...we need to rediscover the mean-
ings of events and the spiritual framework
which our contemporaries have lost.

Precisely! We are a people wandering in a
spiritual wilderness, searching frantically for
our roots and crying out for an understanding
of the context in which we live.

Deeper Issues

If you follow daily headlines you will quickly
conclude that the dominant issues in American
society are economic policy or budget deficits
or social security (in every sense of the term)
or conflicts between conservative and liberal
political philosophies. But these are surface issues.

The deeper issues are first, what values will
we live by—absolute truth, the Holy Word of
God, *or* the arbitrary, relative whims of the
humanist elite? And second, who will set the

moral agenda — the church *or* the bureaucratic social planners and vested economic interests of secular society?

America's moral leadership is up for grabs — and that is where you and I come in. The outcome of today's revolution will be determined by how we respond to the cries of our people for moral direction and vision.

Recent government budget cutbacks put the challenge squarely before us. For fifty years politicians led us to believe that government could provide answers to all social ills. Their recipe was simple: Enact a law, add at least one government agency, pour in money, and stir continuously.

But the ever-spiraling deficit and threat of grave economic consequences shatter that myth. We are learning that there are limits to what we once thought was the endless abundance of the American economy. So government deficits must be curbed, lest the whole system grind to a halt.

But the resulting cutbacks hurt those most dependent on government aid, that is, the poor. Society's concern for its disadvantaged and oppressed is a moral issue. We Christians know from the Old Testament that a people who would sell the poor for a pair of shoes stands in fearsome judgment of Almighty God.

So the government's budget crisis raises a moral dilemma for our society and a spiritual issue for the church. How we respond will say much for the kind of people we are and hope to be; that's why I consider the budget crunch and the plight of the poor "Round Number One" in the battle for America's moral leadership.

The church faced one of its first tests in New York City several years ago, when 36,000 homeless men and women were wandering the city's streets at night. Mayor Edward Koch appealed to religious leaders for help: If each one of New York's 3,500 churches would care for just 10 homeless people, a desperate human problem could be quickly solved—and without huge government expense.

The *New York Times* reported the religious leaders' responses. One Protestant representative was concerned about protocol: "The mayor never mentioned this to me. . . . Nobody in his office called to apprise me of this." A Catholic spokesman sidestepped. A Jewish leader explained that many of the synagogues would not have money for increased heating bills.

The *Times* concluded: The church leaders would need more time to study the mayor's proposal. There was a disturbing silence from evangelicals.

One can almost imagine how it might sound on that day promised in Matthew 25 when our Lord says, "I was a stranger, and you did not invite Me in" (v. 43).

And the religious leaders will respond, "But, Lord, You didn't give us time to study the proposal."

I don't mean to belittle our brothers in New York; the issue is complicated and government cannot immediately transfer to the church full responsibility for the needy. But the sorry response should make us ask ourselves some tough questions. Have we become so caught up in doing our own thing, organizing vast publishing, church, and parachurch empires, that we have lost sight of our biblical mission?

Church bureaucracies can become as bogged down as government bureaucracies, so wrapped up in writing pious statements of faith, issuing press releases, and maintaining property that they forget their reason for existence: to proclaim the Good News and obey the clear commands of the Scriptures.

Of course, the Bible requires justice and righteousness from government, but it also demands that *we* care about our neighbors, clothe the naked, feed the hungry, and visit the sick and those in prison. That's *us* our Lord is talking to, and we don't discharge that obligation by paying our taxes or dropping dimes in charity boxes. We discharge it by *doing* the Word of God.

Amazing things happen when we do exercise our biblical duty. Some time ago we took six convicts, furloughed out of a federal prison in Florida, to Atlanta, where each one was assigned to stay in the home of a Prison Fellowship volunteer. Each morning the six convened for several hours of Bible study, then they converged on the homes of two widows in a deteriorating section of the city. For two weeks they insulated, weatherstripped, caulked, sealed, and painted.

It was all part of a model project demonstrating that nonviolent criminals can do something better than vegetate in a prison cell at a cost to taxpayers averaging $20,000 per year. Without red tape and delays a project valued at $21,000 was completed at no cost to the public. It also proved that people getting busy helping other people can do the job faster and cheaper than cumbersome bureaucracies.

But Atlanta also gave us lessons of far greater significance. I visited one of the widows, Roxie Vaughn, eighty-three years old and blind. When we first told Roxie her home was to be restored, she was elated. Then we told her six prisoners were going to do it, and Roxie turned ashen. You see, she had had some personal experience with crime: Her house had been broken into four times in the prior two years. She had lived in constant fear.

Well, by the third day those prisoners had worked around Roxie's home, she had them in for cookies and milk. The next afternoon television cameras caught a picture of Roxie sitting at her organ playing "Amazing Grace" with those six prisoners around her singing.

I spoke at the service at the end of the project. The widows were there. So were the volunteer families that had hosted the inmates. None of those hosts wanted to see their guests leave. The children were hugging the prisoners; the volunteers were hugging the widows. That dark, musty inner-city sanctuary that hadn't been filled in forty years was jammed full of Christians from all over Atlanta — black and white, rich and poor — in the most exciting and joyous worship imaginable. We were witnessing the incredible power of the Gospel to heal prejudices, to deliver people from fear, and to reconcile us to one another.

Our twentieth-century technology has brought clinical impersonalization: Machines solve all problems; television reduces us all to spectators as life appears in a condensed version from 6 to 7 each evening, in living color. And the by-product of modern technology is the loss of our sense of caring and awareness of one another.

Prison Fellowship recently commissioned researchers to take a comprehensive look at the underlying causes of the rampant juvenile crime sweeping the country. Though their report was substantial, it ultimately reduced the problem to one word: *alienation.* Alienation from self, family, the community, the natural environment, and God.

And the proffered solution? Stable mentors committed to working with youth one-to-one, Christians willing to stand in the gap and bridge the river of alienation that is drowning a new generation.

As we Christians get out of our pews, seek

justice, do the Word of God, and lift up Christ, we will see a sense of community restored to our land.

Think what this can mean for evangelism. The world perceives us as pious and self-centered in our protected sanctuaries and multi-million-dollar church complexes—but that is simply not where most of the sick, hurting, and hungry people are, so they never hear our message. But imagine what would happen if the poor and needy could see us where *they* live, as we meet them at their point of need.

And, if we heed that call, we will be re-asserting a proud heritage of the evangelical church. In the nineteenth century, evangelicals were at the forefront of the most significant social reforms in Western society: enacting child labor laws; ending abuses in the coal mines; establishing public education and public hospitals; and abolishing slavery.

"Round Number One" in the contest for America's moral leadership is still going on; whether the church is willing and able to step up to its biblical responsibility is still to be decided. It may be the greatest question we face. For if we fail even the simple test of responding to human needs in our own community, what possible claim will we have to assume a role of genuine moral leadership in society? We dare not fail.

A Different Kingdom

We are called to live and work and serve in this world but to give our total allegiance to an entirely different kingdom, what the Apostle Peter called the "holy nation."

"You are a chosen race, a royal priesthood, a holy nation, a people for God's own possession, that you may proclaim the excellencies of Him who has called you out of darkness into His marvelous light" (1 Peter 2:9). Peter chose the very words Yahweh used in speaking to Moses on Mount Sinai, when He called His chosen people—the Jews—to be a "holy nation."

Ironic, isn't it, that Peter, the most Jewish of the disciples, the one whom God had to hit over the head three times to get him to bring the Good News to the Gentiles, the one who argued vehemently with Paul that Gentile believers must first become Jews, would be the one to use the term "holy nation," applying what had been the description of the Jews to *all* believers.

But Peter understood that the "holy nation"

was not just another description of the church, but a real nation instituted and bound together by the Holy Creator of heaven and earth, at whose sovereign pleasure all the kingdoms of man are allowed to exist. To understand that we are members of the holy nation should evoke our deepest reverence.

But we live in an age in which the church seems to be beating a steady retreat in the face of the advancing forces of secular culture.

The hard truth is that despite the much-ballyhooed religious resurgence of the seventies and eighties, Christian values are in retreat. We see this most obviously in the erosion of moral values — sexual permissiveness, the blatant parading of perversion, the continued casual disposal of unwanted unborn children, the breakup of the family, the consuming obsession with self and material acquisitions.

Or just look at crime for one example: We incarcerate more people per capita than any nation on earth, yet our murder rate is 2.6 to 8 times higher than that of other industrialized countries. A comparison of murder rates of other nations reveals that Americans between fifteen and twenty-four years of age are being

killed seventy-four times more often than Aus-
trians in that age-group and seventy-three
times more often than Japanese. Murder is
crime to the extreme, but statistics for property crime are abysmal. Ninety-eight percent of
all Americans *will be* crime victims.

And if we are honest, we must admit there's
more of the world in the church than there is
the church in the world.

• A *Christianity Today* survey revealed that
only 26 percent of the general public believed
Jesus Christ to be fully God and fully man;
among evangelicals the response climbed to
only 43 percent.

• In a Gallup survey conducted for Dr. Robert Schuller, 81 percent of those polled said
they considered themselves Christians. But
only 42 percent knew Jesus delivered the Ser-
mon on the Mount—and only 46 percent were
able to name the four Gospels!

• Other Gallup polls revealed that in 1963,
65 percent of the American public believed
the Bible to be infallible; by 1982, that number had declined to 37 percent. In 1992, 32
percent.

• In another survey, 1,382 people were
asked what they considered to be the book

25

that had most influenced them. Fifteen of them cited the Bible—barely more than 1 percent.

In 1976, when my book *Born Again* came out, I appeared on the "Today Show." Barbara Walters held up the book and said, "This is a great book." The next day a reporter asked a presidential candidate campaigning in New Hampshire, "Are you born again?" The obscure governor of Georgia answered, "Yes, I am." He won of course. It was the year of the evangelical. Being born again was fashionable.

Sixteen years later George Gallup asked Americans what institutions they most fear. The response? Fifty percent said they feared fundamentalists, while only 38 percent feared secular humanists.

We've gone from being the most fashionable group in America to being the most feared.

So it has never been more important—or, indeed, more difficult—for American Christians to understand what our citizenship in the "holy nation" means.

Eternal Citizenship

First, we must recognize that our eternal citizenship is in the kingdom of God, as clearly stated by Paul in Philippians 3:20. We are but sojourners in this nation, beloved though it is. We are clearly commanded by our Lord to seek *first* the kingdom of God (Matthew 6:33).

Many of us are frustrated by apostasy and declining morality in America today. It is evident on all sides. It's no wonder that Christians today yearn for the good ol' days of moral absolutes, when young people prayed in schools, parents retained authority over their children, folks loved their country and respected one another's property, and life was so much simpler.

Many of our brothers and sisters have decided to get involved; the most dramatic change in the American religious scene in the 1980s was the emergence of fundamentalist churches into the political arena. Notoriously separatist in the past, concerned primarily with protecting their own piety against the contaminating influences of the outside, those churches made a conscious effort to lead a Christian crusade to restore morality to America.

Indeed, the decay of American culture demands our involvement. There must be a Christian influence in every facet of society. Christians must participate, vote, work from within and without to see that government is an instrument of social justice.

But too there are grave pitfalls of failing to make clear the distinction between the holy nation and the nation-state. Christian moral and political movements, undertaken beneath the banner of simplistic God and country clichés, run this risk. Let me explain:

• First, no matter how well-motivated they are, some so-called Christian movements use God to sanctify the political prejudices of their adherents. And politicians are often willing partners in the process; I can testify from personal experience that politicians are not above using religious movements to their own advantage. The danger is that whenever we tie the Gospel to the political fortunes of any person or party, it is the Gospel that is made hostage and the Gospel that suffers.

• Second, Christian political movements can become exclusive. No one agenda can fit all moral situations.

Let us never limit God. He may burden you with one particular cause. He may burden me with another. In fact, I suspect that He assigns burdens and responsibilities throughout His kingdom; what might be on my agenda will not necessarily fit another equally dedicated Christian's agenda. The only absolute agenda is the uncompromising standard of righteousness and justice that Almighty God has woven through every page of His Holy Word.

• Third, in our passion to scrub America clean of its most obvious vices — homosexuality, abortion, pornography, etc. — we narrow the scope of Christian concern. And, by our silence, we implicitly embrace those things not on our hit list, aligning ourselves with the subtle sins of privilege, power, conspicuous affluence. We do it in a way our Lord very pointedly eschewed.

The American church, fairly or unfairly, is perceived as a white, Anglo-Saxon, upper-middle-class phenomenon. The same folks who dine at the country club on Saturday evenings, rub shoulders on padded pews at their gilded churches on Sunday mornings. The danger is that we become so identified with an affluent American lifestyle, that people who can't or won't accept the values of that culture can't or won't accept the Gospel of Christ.

Time after time I find that men and women in the prisons of America want nothing to do with the church or with Christianity. They cannot relate to our lavish buildings and stained-glass windows because they see the church as a manifestation of the culture that has rejected them and holds them prisoner.

But I see those same people come alive when I talk about Jesus the prisoner, the outcast who was followed by a dirty dozen, the One who was laid in a borrowed manger, rode on a borrowed donkey, was arrested, hung on a cross between two thieves, and then buried in a borrowed tomb. They can understand and identify with the Jesus of the Scriptures, not with a Christ who appears to have just stepped out of a Brooks Brothers catalog.

The longer I'm a Christian, the more I realize that the vague deity of American civil religion is a heretical rejection of the Christ of Holy Scripture. So don't confuse your loyalties—never assume the will of the majority and the will of God are synonymous. They may be different—and frequently are.

The Christian is committed to work for justice and righteousness, to bring the Gospel of Christ to bear in all areas of life to make a difference in society. But we do it by the integrity of our witness, not by resorting to quick, simplistic clichés.

Community

Second, as citizens of the holy nation, we necessarily and automatically become part of a community beyond ourselves. Many Christians think of conversion as personal and private. But being converted is not just being separated—or "saved"—from one's sinful past; it is being joined to a holy God and His people. That is the very essence of the covenant.

That sounds simple, but living it is not. Ours is a conspicuously egocentric era, preoccupied with our individual fulfillment and success. And I fear for the next generation—which is growing up in front of video games instead of basketball hoops or pitchers' mounds. Fifty percent of Americans watch television as they're eating dinner. So much for family conversation.

Our video and computer games are a form of electronic solitaire, as if 230 million people had so lost their capacity to relate to one another that they are more comfortable staring at twelve-inch screens shooting fake airplanes out of the air than they are looking at one another. With the prevalence of VCRs and videos, we don't even communally watch movies anymore. We prefer the couch-potato life.

We Christians must be different, prepared to live not by the self-aggrandizing rules of this culture, but by that commandment that tells us to bear one another's burdens and to lay down our lives for one another. Let me illustrate:

• Next to my conversion, the most powerful spiritual experience of my life was when, in prison, I learned that a member of my prayer group—who happened then to be the eighth-ranking Republican in the House of Representatives, now the former governor of Minnesota—had asked the President if he could serve out my remaining sentence so I could be with my wife and kids, who were experiencing serious problems. *That is citizenship in the holy nation.*

• For ten years a couple in Ohio faithfully corresponded with and periodically visited a Christian inmate who finally came up for parole. Obie hadn't been "out" in twenty years. He was sixty-one years old and apprehensive, even terrified, about the transition. How did the couple—Denny and Betty Nagy—respond? They drove across the state, picked him up at the gate, and took him to his new neighborhood—their neighborhood, where "family" could stand by for support. And there's more to the story: The Nagys hadn't stood alone in their ministry to Obie. For some years their church had paid travel and phone expenses. As Obie moved to the community, the church rallied forces to help him find employment. *That's citizenship in the holy nation.*

Since we are a part of a corporate body, we bear corporate responsibility for what happens around us. All too often we Christians act as if we secretly delight in the moral pollution around us; the more depraved the world is, the more righteous we feel by comparison.

That can be very dangerous. Remember Nehemiah: Before he undertook the extraordinary task of rebuilding the walls of Jerusalem, he prayed that God would forgive him his sins . . . *and the sins of his fathers* (1:6). When God's judgment comes on a people, it comes upon the just as well as the unjust.

When overworked doctors in a clinic in Chicago could not take time between abortions to fill out the forms for payment, they made hatch marks on their bloodstained smocks, casually totaling them up at the end of each day. We recoil in horror, relieved that we are not part of such a desecration of God's creation. But of course we are—inescapably so. We of the holy nation within the nation-state need to be a deeply repentant people whose hearts are contrite, whose hearts break over the practices of our culture that break the heart of God.

Worship

Third, as members of the holy nation, we worship the unseen God, who through His Son dwells in each of us. We are to respect and follow those in whom God reposes spiritual authority, but we must remember that ours is a jealous Sovereign. The first four of the Ten Commandments deal not with our sins against our fellowman but with the requirements of exclusive worship and reverence for our Creator God.

A *USA Today* poll asked people why they went to church. Forty-five percent said they went because it was good for them. "Worship" didn't even rate in the survey report. We need to rediscover the first line of an old gospel song: "I stand amazed in the presence of Jesus the Nazarene."

We Americans stand amazed in the presence

of fame for fame's sake. To be the object of adulation and worship in America, one needs only to appear frequently enough on television to be generally recognized; it has nothing to do with why the person is famous. As British journalist Henry Fairlie said,

> We say correctly of some people that they idolize success, but our societies as a whole also worship it, and again the celebrity is a symbol. We do not applaud his talents, even if he should have any; we applaud his success.

Just look at the utterly idolatrous worship of Elvis Presley. A $500,000 collection of Presley artifacts toured the country some years ago, attracting as many as 200,000 viewers at each stop. The display manager, who spent $1,000 for one of the most popular items—a pair of Presley's underpants—told reporters, "I almost didn't buy them...but the women just went nuts over them, wanted their pictures taken with them." Millions of Americans fanatically worship the memory of this dead man who would hole up for months eating compulsively, ogling porno films, who was so stoned much of the time that he couldn't control his bowels during the night. That we have so extolled this pathetic man says more about us than Presley. As Shakespeare wrote in *Macbeth*, "Fair is foul and foul is fair." Similarly, the Bible says, "Woe to those who call evil good, and good evil" (Isaiah 5:20) and to those "whose god is their appetite, and whose glory is in their shame, who set their minds on earthly things" (Philippians 3:19). The very next verse presents the contrast: But "our citizenship is in heaven." We are to be different—daringly different.

What is it about us that causes us to withhold from God the reverence we lavish on human idols? Over and over in the White House, I met people who would fiercely complain about a policy and demand an audience with the President. But the roaring lions I escorted from the waiting room became meek lambs in the Oval Office. I saw more awe in that one room than I have seen in the sanctuaries of all our churches combined.

But that is the secular world, you say. Well, that same attitude has captured much of the Christian world. Instead of the pelvis-grinding rendition of "Hound Dog," we Christians have substituted Pepsodent smiles, sprayed-stiff hair, and syrupy baritones, all slickly directed before expensive video cameras. But just because we're electronically as good as Johnny Carson doesn't mean that we are penetrating the world with the convicting message of Christ.

The Word

Fourth, as citizens of the holy nation, we take our stand not on the shifting sands of secular relativism but on the holy and inerrant Word of God. Decisions in the world are made on the basis of expedience and changing sociological factors.

As for our government's shifting sands, I offer two opinions from the Supreme Court that show how the federal government officially views religion. The first, from 1933: "The essence of religion is belief in a relation to God involving duties superior to those arising from any human relation." I'll buy that.

But during the turmoil of the 1960s, the Court saw fit to give us a new definition of religion: "A sincere and meaningful belief which occupies in the life of its possessor a place parallel to that filled by God of those admittedly qualifying for this [conscientious] exemption."

In other words, in the eyes of the government, one certainly does not need God to be religious; if one is occupied by a sincere and meaningful belief in a tuna fish, perhaps, that will do just fine.

But as citizens of the kingdom of God, we stand on the unchanging, immutable Word of God. Without it, we Christians have nothing.

Taking our stand on biblical truth can be our only defense against our culture's penchant to reduce all issues to simplistic suppositions and glib answers. We impatiently expect to get solutions to the most profound ambiguities of life the same way we drive up to the fast-food counter: one double burger, chocolate shake, and an order of fries. We are faddists. Just look at the rash of new diets and instant physical-conditioning courses that week after week dominate our bestseller lists.

The problem is, that "easy-answer" mentality is invading the Christian church: We want scorecards by which we can instantly rate our politicians, new catch acronyms for salvation, time-saving techniques for discipleship. But formulas don't convert people; slick slogans and cute phrases are no substitute for hard spiritual truth.

In our well-intentioned effort to reach unsaved masses, we often make the Gospel message itself sound easy, unthreatening, a painless answer to all life's ills. We portray a loving God who forgives all and asks nothing in return. Now, that may tickle the ears of this pleasure-seeking generation, but it is nothing less than heresy.

As citizens in the holy nation, we must challenge presuppositions — not only of society as a whole but of the evangelical subculture as well. The Gospel of Jesus Christ must be the bad news of the conviction of sin before it can be the Good News of redemption.

Some years ago I was with Billy Graham who admonished me to follow his example in this regard: Every time he preaches he reads one particular verse, "For all have sinned and fall short of the glory of God" (Romans 3:23).

On "60 Minutes" Mike Wallace once interviewed a survivor of Auschwitz, a key witness against Adolf Eichmann, the mastermind of the Holocaust. Upon entering the courtroom and facing Eichmann, this witness began to tremble. Weeping uncontrollably, he collapsed.

When Mike Wallace asked this man why he had collapsed—was it reliving the memories, the nightmares, and the griefs?—the man answered: "No. I collapsed because I was afraid about myself. I saw that I am exactly like him, capable of this."

Now I've been interviewed by Mike Wallace and he's a pro. It's hard to shake him, but this answer did. He almost couldn't ask the next question. He stared at the man, then turned to the camera and said, "That poses a question. Was Eichmann a monster, a mad man, or something even more terrifying? Was he normal?"

All have sinned. The Word of God proclaims it and the Word of God stands, despite the prevalent myth of the twentieth century—that man is by nature good.

In 1981 a very readable little book was published with the appealing title *When Bad Things Happen to Good People*. Written by a Boston rabbi, Harold Kushner, it was an overnight sensation, fifty-two weeks on the *New York Times* bestseller list, millions of copies sold. The title of the book implies that if things go "wrong," it can't be our own fault. There has to be an explanation. What can it be?

Kushner's thesis is simple enough: God is all-loving but not all-powerful; the bad things that happen to us are out of His control. So the rabbi exhorts his readers to "learn to love and forgive Him [God] despite His limitations."

Now it will be immediately obvious to you that this god of Kushner's is not the God of Abraham and of Israel, not the all-powerful God revealed in the Scriptures.

But you may say, so what? If one rabbi rejects Jewish orthodoxy and writes a book offering easy answers to life's great mysteries and a hungry and hurting people gobble it up, what's the surprise?

Well, if that were the whole story, you'd be right. But there's more.

The book jacket carried the ringing endorsements of one of America's leading Christian personalities, as well as a seminary professor. It was widely distributed in Christian churches; in fact, I finally decided to read it only after a dozen or more evangelicals recommended it to me. Pastors preached from it. It was a big seller in many Christian bookstores.

When I looked around for critical comment I found only a few Christian publications negatively reviewing the book; others were silent.

Even Rabbi Kushner said he was surprised his book had not received more criticism. When I wrote a critical article about the book for Prison Fellowship's *Jubilee* newsletter, I was deluged with mail, most of it saying, "Amen, someone's finally speaking out." But several pastors angrily denounced me for challenging a book they had found "comforting to their congregations."

"Comforting?" Indeed. So might doses of narcotics be comforting.

Kushner's book wasn't just the skewed theology of one rabbi; it was — and is — a national phenomenon, one of the most significant books in several years, enormously influencing our culture's perception of God. And we Christians went right along with the game, embracing it, even promoting it. My friends, that is not just buying into the errors of the secular culture; it is not a slight compromise with so-called realism. It is treachery to God; it is changing sides in the battle; it is promoting blasphemy. It is throwing aside the Word of God rather than standing on it as our authority.

And Kushner's book is not, I'm sorry to say, the only example. Whatever is hot in America's pop culture finds its way into the Christian market dressed in evangelical jargon. Many Christian "how-to" books, records, and tapes simply tell us how to use God as a lever to get whatever it is we desire. Get thin. Get successful. Get rich. Such religious adaptions of the self-indulgent, egocentric, materialistic culture are not only Jesus-justified hedonism but dreadful heresy—for they suggest that the majestic Creator God of this universe exists for man's pleasure rather than vice versa.

So it is that we have, I fear, slipped unknowingly into a state of moral paralysis. We are so comfortable with the "comforting" world's ways that we no longer are able to discern what is false and what is true. We have forgotten that moral confusion is the enemy's favorite weapon.

For Satan comes not in a red suit carrying a pitchfork; rather, as Shakespeare wrote in *King Lear*, the devil is a gentleman. Before his fall he was called Lucifer, the angel of light and knowledge; in the Garden of Eden, he was the most attractive of all the animals. And today he cloaks his propaganda in the conventional wisdom of the times—the rights of men and women to pursue the pleasure principle first articulated by John Stuart Mill. The pursuit of happiness, immediate and temporal, has become a moral obligation.

And the deceiver uses the bludgeon sparingly, preferring little subtleties, inferences, and suggestions which slip through the lines of Christian defenses, then over time establish themselves as legitimate. It's an insidious process of gradual compromise that has nothing to do with living as a citizen of heaven, in disciplined submission to the Word of God.

We must point people to the Holy Bible in their search for truth and answers. We who follow Christ must take our stand the only place we can—on the holy, infallible Word of God. We don't have anything else.

I use the word "infallible" advisedly. There is no issue I've wrestled with harder since I've been a Christian than my view of the Scriptures. My lawyer's mind demanded evidence before I could believe the Bible to be without error. But the more I probed, the clearer that truth became. Ironically, it was as a result of my Watergate experiences that I became utterly convinced that the Bible is absolutely authoritative—God's inerrant revelation. Life can be lived only in absolute and disciplined submission to its authority.

Righteous Living

Fifth, we are commanded to seek first not only the kingdom of God — don't stop there — but His righteousness as well.

Righteousness or holy living is often seen by Christians as maintaining chaste sexual standards, tithing, faithful church attendance, being friendly to those around us. Well, those are indeed Christian responsibilities, but only the beginning of holy living.

And many believers categorize their refraining from alcohol, tobacco, cards, and dancing as holy living. Though God may call you to that type of witness, it is only skimming the surface at best. That is piety. And we must never, never confuse piety with righteousness.

Righteousness was defined by Yahweh at Mount Sinai and interpreted by the fiery words of His prophets from Isaiah to Amos to Habakkuk and, ultimately, by the life of His Son, Jesus. God's definition of righteousness is based on justice for all people, especially the unfortunate: You shall not sell the poor for a pair of shoes, nor take away the coat of a man who borrows from you; you shall pay your employees a just wage; you shall care for widows and orphans; you shall hate evil and do good. "Remodel your courts into true halls of justice," thundered the Prophet Amos (see Amos 5:15). "Let justice roll down like waters and righteousness like an ever-flowing stream" (v. 24). That's God's standard of righteousness and holy living.

After ten years in a Soviet gulag, Alexander Solzhenitsyn wrote, "Bless you, prison, for having been in my life." For it was there he learned that "the meaning of earthly existence lies, not as we have grown used to thinking, in prospering, but in the development of the soul." I too can say, "Bless you prison," for it was there that I learned to see justice in the way that Amos and Micah and Jeremiah and Isaiah saw it, the way it is to be in the holy nation.

When I was in law and politics, I believed justice was determined by a majority vote, 50 percent plus one. Justice was simply the law, which I tried to influence, often on behalf of very affluent clients. In the White House I saw justice as the sum of rules and policies that I tried to shape, often on behalf of those people whose influence—or campaign contribution—

was significant enough to get them past the White House gates and into my office.

Then too I had grown up in the insecurity of the Depression, believing deeply in the work ethic; justice was also protecting individual's earnings and keeping the government from interfering with their rights.

Finally, of course, justice was the instrument for punishing and removing from society those who refused — or were unable — to live by the rules that people like myself made.

But from a prison cell I saw men condemned to waste away for long years — for what seemed like trivial offenses. Like most people, I had thought prisons were populated by violent, dangerous criminals. What a shock to find that the man in the bunk next to me was a former bank vice-president who battled the government for nine years over $3,000 of tax evasion. For a first offense, he received a three-year sentence. I found young men who couldn't afford lawyers. I found others who were sentenced without knowing why — or for how long. It was in a prison cell that I came to understand why God makes special demands on His people to care for the oppressed, sick, suffering, and needy.

Justice is not achieved in God's eyes until a society is as concerned with the rights and dignity of the person in a prison cell as it is with the one in the executive suite.

If we're honest, I suspect we will agree that we're as far away from that standard today as the holy nation was in the time of Amos. But that standard is what you and I must work for.

Obedience

Sixth, we must be prepared as citizens of the holy nation to take our stand in faithful obedience to our Lord, to make a difference with our lives. That will probably mean standing against the culture in "a bold and majestic witness to the holy commandments of God," as Carl Henry has put it. That does not just mean contributing or paying dues to some moralistic crusade. It means standing in the gap, if need be, by yourself.

The late Francis Schaeffer once wrote and told me of meeting believers in various walks of life whose Christian faith was making absolutely no difference in their vocations. He concluded,

We talk a lot about the need of having true Christians getting into the media, the chaplaincy, etc. . . . but there is no use for our people getting into the media or the chaplaincy or anything else unless they are willing for confrontation when necessary, even when it is costly to their careers.

Exactly right. Let me give you one illustration — there are many — of what it can mean for a Christian to take his stand against the culture.

In 1977 Harry Fred Palmer, a Vietnam veteran, was arrested in Elkhart, Indiana for burglary; while in jail awaiting trial he accepted Christ. His offense carried a mandatory minimum sentence of ten years — although that law, acknowledged as arbitrary by the legislature, had been changed eighteen days after Palmer's arrest.

The judge assigned to the case, William Bontrager, had himself been converted to Christ recently. He reviewed the facts, concluded the ten-year minimum statute unconstitutional, and sentenced Palmer to one year in prison with the provision he thereafter make restitution to those he had robbed, and perform community service.

Palmer did just that. He served his year, a model prisoner, active in Prison Fellowship programs. After his release he began paying back his victims and was reunited with his wife and family. The case was a model of justice, restitution, and restoration.

But the Indiana Supreme Court swung into action, claiming that Bontrager's suspension of the mandatory sentence was unconstitutional. Palmer should serve the remaining nine years of his automatic sentence, they said, even though the law requiring it was no longer in existence. They ordered Bontrager to send him back to jail.

For Bontrager, the court's order was clearly a case of choosing to obey the law of man or the law of God. He had been reading the Old Testament prophets; God's demands for justice and righteousness had seared his conscience. He knew the Supreme Court's order would serve neither, merely a technicality of the law.

So he disqualified himself, turning the case over to another judge. A nightmarish sequence of events followed. The court slammed Palmer back behind bars, declared Bontrager in contempt, fined him $500, and sentenced him to thirty days in prison. Though that sentence was suspended, the court began proceedings to remove him from the bench. Rather than allow his own struggle to endanger Palmer's chance for appeals, Judge Bontrager resigned.

It was not a painless decision. He gave up a comfortable salary, the judgeship he had worked all his life to attain, and the security of community respect. But Judge Bontrager's spiritual discernment was keen — he knew to send a man back to prison for a debt he had already paid was at odds with the standard of justice of the holy God he served. So he had to take his stand — whatever the cost.

Though your arena may not be the courtroom, I guarantee you will have many opportunities, small and large, to take your stand. If not, you need to question your own commitment. Conformity is the high priest of American culture and has infiltrated the holy nation.

We live in an age in which compromise is applauded as one of the highest virtues of civilized men. Our pluralistic form of government uses compromise to make an issue acceptable to the greatest number of people by a process of negotiation.

But what may occasionally work in the secular world is not necessarily God's wisdom. A compromise of hot and cold yields lukewarm. And God, speaking in Revelation, is resolute about lukewarmness: "I know your deeds, that you are neither cold nor hot. . . . So because you are lukewarm, and neither hot nor cold, I will spit you out of My mouth" (3:15-16).

It is not easy, but, I beseech you, *dare to be different.* Dare to live as a citizen of the holy nation.

Time for Action

Seventh, and finally, citizens of the holy nation must participate in the human drama. Much of the church today has withdrawn, seeking refuge on the high ground. Our multi-million-dollar church complexes surrounded by acres of paved parking lots are as remote and protected as walled medieval fortresses, protected from the swirling waters where most of the sick, hungry, and hurting people are. So those in need cannot identify with us and will consequently never hear our message. But imagine what would happen if they see us where they live, as we met them at their point of need.

Jacques Ellul wrote that until we have

really understood the actual plight of our contemporaries and we have heard their cry of anguish, until we have shared their suffering both physical and spiritual, and their despair and desolation, then we shall be able to proclaim the Word of God, but not until then.

The Apostle Paul called it the fellowship of suffering (Philippians 3:10). It is a spiritual mystery—suffering with others draws us closer to our Christ who suffered for us. Being in prison has given me this insight. For the most meaningful communions I have had with my Lord have not been in the great cathedrals of the world I've been privileged to preach in nor in the parliaments where I have spoken nor in the most influential gatherings of Christian leaders. They have been instead on my knees on the grimy, concrete floor of a rotten prison cell with my hand on the shoulder of a tough convict who sobs with joy as we meet Another who was in prison, executed, and rose from a tomb for us—His name is Jesus.

My friends, take your posts. You have been called out by the most high and holy God to serve Him in the building of His holy nation.

You are called not to be successful or to meet any of the other counterfeit standards of this world, but to be faithful and to be expended in the cause of serving the risen and returning Christ.

CHAPTER TWO

The Role of the Church in Society

T he role of the church in American life is being debated today as never before. And the debate has crucial consequences for those of us who call ourselves followers of Jesus Christ.

The relationship between church and state has always been a serious issue. In the first century, Christians in Rome refused to give Caesar equal billing with God. Not that they wouldn't respect Caesar; they simply wouldn't call him Lord, and for that they were thrown to the lions.

Then Emperor Constantine became a Christian and instituted the Holy Roman Empire; from then on — and for centuries afterward in Europe — nations were "Christian" nations. Church and state merged together, vying for power.

In fact, what distinguished American colonists hundreds of years later was that they were determined to provide religious freedom for every citizen. They developed a system of pluralism and, interestingly enough, it was a Christian who argued in the beginning of our nation that the state cannot convert; only the power of God can.

Distorted Pictures

My heart grieves when I read how the press talks about the church today. (I suppose the confusion is understandable: According to one survey only 8 percent of the secular press corps attend church regularly; so when they discuss spiritual issues, it's a little like calling in a team of plumbers to perform open-heart surgery.) Look at some of the religious issues misunderstood by the press:

- The first is that the church (particularly

the fundamentalist church) is going to rise up and take over America. But can you imagine the church of Jesus Christ, which can't even agree on how to interpret the Bible, having the power to take over this country? In our current fractured state, we don't have the power to take over this country. Nor do we have the disposition to do it; God provides the Spirit who will change people, not the state.

• The second nonsense that we hear today is this question of separation of church and state. The term *separation of church and state* was never even considered when the Constitution was written. It was introduced fifteen years later by Thomas Jefferson. And the separation that the founders talked about was keeping the state out of the church, not keeping the church out of the religious and moral welfare of the country. They certainly never intended that religious influence be erased from our society.

Indeed, the founding fathers based our country on Judeo-Christian beliefs and principles, and if you look through the pages of American history, what a proud tradition we Christians have. Again, Christians of the early nineteenth century were at the forefront of founding public hospitals and public education, of meeting human needs, and stopping abuses of working men and women. The abolition of slavery was spearheaded by Christians, as was the civil rights movement. Don't tell me that religion doesn't belong in public life. You bet it does, because it's been for the moral betterment of our country.

• The third area of confusion is the great political debate between conservatives and liberals that threatens to polarize America and with it the church of Jesus Christ. The conservative argument is, "Bring America back to God and old-fashioned values." Certainly, I am all for bringing America back to its traditional values. But I think there is a grave danger when we begin to talk that way, for it would amount to creating civil religion in this land, that is, putting the state and God on the same basis. One recent President put it very well. He said American government makes no sense unless it is founded on a deeply felt religious faith, and "I don't care what it is." You see, that's faith in faith. It's civil religion. It's a belief that God and country are equal. And it's very dangerous.

On the other side of the political spectrum,

liberals say that religion is intensely personal and should have no effect on public policy. New York Governor Mario Cuomo remarked in a speech at the University of Notre Dame that, as a Christian, he believed abortion was wrong and the teaching of the church was right, but as long as a majority of the citizens of his state did not favor that position, he was not morally obligated to carry it out. In essence, Cuomo said, "God speaks truth but it has to be ratified by a majority vote of the people."

That's wrong. That kind of speech gives sophistry a bad name. Yet how did the press characterize Governor Cuomo's speech? One reporter wrote, "At last someone has cleared away all of the confusion and given us an intelligent position we can believe in." Of course, it is an intelligent position to the secular press because it denies the authority of God over our lives.

We Christians must now more than ever proclaim that Jesus Christ is Lord over all political structures. The values of the Gospel of Jesus Christ must never be held hostage to the fortune of any political party or individual.

But the issues being debated today in the press raise another question, much more fundamental than just the relationship of church and state. They raise a question about how our secular culture perceives the church. What do people really see? If you want to know something about water, the last creature you ask is a fish, because he lives in it. And if you want to know about the church, I guess the last people you really ought to ask are Christians, because we are in it and we don't really see how the world sees us.

The *Washington Post* recently featured a front-page article that characterized evangelical Christians as "largely poor, uneducated, and easy to command." If a journalist said that about any other group in America, he would be fired on the spot, but the *Post* didn't fire anyone. It merely expressed surprise that many readers found the description offensive. A few days later, one of the bemused editors explained that they felt they were simply printing something that is "universally accepted."

That illustration is a sorry example of how we evangelicals are perceived by the press.

I give three critical mistakes the world makes when it looks at the church of Jesus Christ. Are we responsible for these misguided views?

Just a Building?

The first is that when people look at the church, they tend to see a building, a physical structure — a misconception I think Christians have encouraged. How many times have you heard people say, "Let's go to church"? First-century believers didn't say, "We're going to church." They said, "We *are* the church."

The church of Jesus Christ is us! Don't speak of it as a building. Jesus never did. Jesus never said, "Come to the temple." Instead, He commanded the church, "Go! Preach the Gospel! Make disciples! Go into all the world!"

The Greek word for "church" is *ecclesia*. Not a building, not an edifice, but a gathering, an assembly of people. Actually, the first Christians were forbidden to construct buildings for worship.

Several years ago I had the opportunity to preach in the Full Gospel Church of Seoul, Korea. There were 10,000 people in the sanctuary, 15,000 in the overflow halls, six services on that Sunday. It was not the numbers that moved me; rather, I was overwhelmed by the presence of the Spirit. Afterward I told the pastor how excited I was about his church. He said, "Oh, this isn't the church; this is just where we gather Sunday morning. The church, you see, is in the home — 10,000 homes all across Seoul where members meet every morning for two hours of Bible study and prayer."

Then I understood why in that country of 35 million Buddhists and only 2 million evangelical Christians, Christian values dominate the culture. It is because Korean Christians take their faith seriously. We in this supposedly Christian nation, but one in which humanist values dominate, desperately need to learn from our Korean brothers and sisters.

The danger of thinking of the church as a building is that whenever we do, we render ourselves powerless in society.

During the 1977 energy crisis, the Commonwealth of Virginia ordered all nonessential buildings closed. Number one on the list? The church. Nonessential. All you do is open it on Sunday morning for people to come in, sit, and be entertained, and the rest of the week it sits empty. "Close the church to save energy." That's what the governor said. His fault or ours?

In Washington, D.C., one local church was

in legal "hot water" for taking in homeless people and allowing them to spend the night. The zoning authority said that that was a violation of city ordinances because the function of a church was Sunday morning worship, not giving people a place to sleep.

Slowly but surely, people are viewing the church as having a narrow, limited function, and we're lending that attitude a hand by boxing ourselves in. The great Archbishop of Canterbury William Temple (1881–1944) once said that the church of Jesus Christ is the only cooperative society that exists for the benefit of its *non*members. We're to take the church out of the walls of our sanctuaries and to the people.

Wherever a repressive regime has tried to destroy the church, it has tried to prevent Christians from reaching out to people.

In 1929, when the Soviet government wanted to wipe out the church, what did they do? They passed a law, not to close the orthodox church buildings and prohibit meetings on Sunday morning, but to make it a crime to conduct church school, to help the poor, to go into the neighborhoods and reach out to people. Believers had to stay within their churches on Sunday morning. What the Soviet Communists did *by decree* in 1929, we are allowing to be done to us today *by default.*

What a difference the church makes when we move out into society:

• When I visited the New Mexico State Penitentiary, I was excited to discover that all six men on death row were Christians who loved the Lord. The youngest, only eighteen years old, said to me, "I'm ready to die; I'm ready to be with Jesus." He continued, "But before I die I want to make a film on the problem of child sexual molestation, because I am a victim. I want to leave something that will be shown in schools to tell kids how to deal with it." The church was there in that prison because volunteers had gone in and taken the Good News to men condemned to die.

• During a Prison Fellowship seminar in a Kentucky prison, eight prisoners walked to the front of the chapel and made professions of faith in Christ. More than fifty other inmates and fifteen Prison Fellowship volunteers looked on with pride and excitement. Afterward, three inmates filled a large, galvinized horse trough in the prison yard with water, and the church gathered around it for an impromptu baptism service.

As the chaplain led each of the new Christians into the water, most wept; the eyes of their brothers in Christ and the volunteers also filled with tears. A softball game in the prison yard broke up, and the players and many others stood watching intently. A few jeered, but they were ignored. All eyes were on the eight men, who before this day had stood for nothing but wrong. Now, because of Christ, they had the courage to take a stand for Him in prison — where doing so is not only a witness, but a risk.

• Some years ago I met Jack Eckerd, the founder of Eckerd Drug Stores. We began to talk about the Christian faith, and several months later Jack Eckerd gave his life to the Lord. The first thing he did was walk into one of his 1,500 stores and see *Playboy* and *Penthouse* magazines on the bookshelves. He went back to his store managers and said, "This is wrong. We shouldn't be selling *Playboy* and *Penthouse* here. Take those magazines out of my stores."

The managers protested, "We're making a huge profit selling those magazines."

Jack Eckerd replied, "I don't care. Take those magazines out of my stores."

Now you can walk into an Eckerd Drug Store anywhere in the United States and you will find that the shelves once filled with pornography are now clean of it. As other Christians across the country voiced their protests, other chains followed suit—taking those magazines out of sight if not off the shelves completely.

• In Belfast, Northern Ireland, where the streets are torn almost daily by the bomb blasts of sectarian strife, the drama of reconciliation has taken place in the most unlikely place—the prisons. I've seen this restoration and healing firsthand. At a Prison Fellowship International conference in Belfast, we were joined by two young prisoners—Liam, a Roman Catholic, and Jimmy, a Protestant.

Liam had been the last member of the famous Maze Prison hunger strikes some years ago in which Bobby Sands led nearly a dozen fellow terrorists to their deaths. When Liam's turn came, he starved himself for fifty-five days. Blind, weak, and near death, he was visited by his mother, who convinced him to break the fast. During Liam's recovery, he realized he had to make a choice between his cause—the Irish Republican Army—and Jesus Christ.

He chose Christ—and from that point on, his faith led him to radical steps of forgiveness and love.

He began eating with his former enemies, breaking the strict segregation between Catholics and Protestants in his prison mess hall. And eventually, through Liam's witness, Jimmy, a Protestant ex-terrorist, came to know Christ. Furloughed for the week of our conference, the two stood on a stage before a huge crowd of both Catholics and Protestants. As Liam put his arm around Jimmy's shoulders, he evidenced the power of the Christ who reconciles: "Before, if I had seen Jimmy on the street," he said, "I would have shot him. Now he's my brother in Christ. I would die for him!"

● When Peru's Lurangancho Prison was known as the worst prison in the world, I visited—after a nun had been killed there and all religious workers had been barred (though Prison Fellowship volunteers were still going in). When I walked into one of the cell blocks, the smell was so putrid it was overpowering. I started to slide on the floor, and I looked down to find I was walking on sewage overflowing from each cell.

Yet at every fourth or fifth cell in that terrible place, a man would grab me by the sleeve, pull me into his cell, and with a beaming smile point to a Prison Fellowship discipleship seminar certificate hanging on the wall. A bit later, an older man grabbed my hand. He was hot and sweaty, and started to cry. He said in broken English, "You great man because you come and you love us." I wrapped my arms around him and let him cry on my shoulder. There in that awful pit of perversity and despair, men are coming to know the glory of Jesus Christ because the church has been there.

Indeed, our job is to go into those places in our society where people need to be restored; that's where you see the kingdom of God being built. When that is our witness, people can't say we're cloistered in our marble and glass cathedrals, but that we're out in the world, living the faith.

Just a Self-help Group?

The second error the world makes when it looks at the church today is seeing us as just another competitor in the free American market of self-improvement schemes. To unbelievers, we're a little bit like est or mind control or yoga—"If it makes you feel better to put God on your side, do it."

I picked up a newspaper some time ago and the thought for the day on the editorial page quoted a prominent American pastor as saying: "Put God to work for you and maximize your potential in this divinely ordered capitalistic system." That's not only cheap grace and bad theology, it's heresy. God was not made for our benefit; we were made for His pleasure. The church does not exist to make people happy; the church is here to make people holy.

Yet too often the message we are preaching today is not the convicting news of sin and salvation through none but Jesus Christ; instead, it is, "Come to God and be showered with blessings."

Martin Luther saw things differently. He said, "I have followed the rule not to minister comfort to any person except those who have become contrite and are sorrowing because of their sin. Those who have despaired of self help."

What does the Bible tell us about our duty as Christians? The Apostle Paul wrote to his disciple Timothy,

All Scripture is inspired by God and profitable for teaching, for reproof, for correction, for training in righteousness; that the man of God may be adequate, equipped for every good work. I solemnly charge you in the presence of God and of Christ Jesus, who is to judge the living and the dead, and by His appearing and His kingdom: preach the Word; be ready in season and out of season; reprove, rebuke, exhort, with great patience and instruction (2 Timothy 3:16–4:2).

When I became a Christian, the first thing I did was pick up a Bible. I'm a lawyer, and my lawyer's mind demanded evidence. Is this Book really the Word of God that it claims to be, or is it a collection of legends? So I read it from cover to cover; I also read books about the Bible. I learned, for example, that the Psalms were indeed written when they said they were written. Until recent years, higher critics of Holy Scripture had claimed that the prophecy of Jesus Christ's crucifixion which is given in meticulous detail in Psalm 22 could only have been written a hundred years before His time since the torture of crucifixion hadn't even been invented at the time of David. Then the Dead Sea Scrolls confirmed what believers in an infallible, inerrant Bible have always said to be so.

I also closely examined what Jesus said about Scripture and about Himself. Go through the New Testament sometime and see how He always quoted the Old Testament as the Word of God. When Christ resisted the devil in the wilderness, three times He quoted from the Law, "It is written" (Matthew 4:4, 7, 10; cf. Deuteronomy 8:3; 6:16, 13). When He spoke to the two disciples on the road to Emmaus following His resurrection, He said,

"O foolish men and slow of heart to believe in all that the prophets have spoken! Was it not necessary for the Christ to suffer these things and to enter into His glory?" And beginning with Moses and with all the prophets, He explained to them the things concerning Himself in all the Scriptures (Luke 24:25-27).

Jesus also said, "Thy Word is truth" (John 17:17), and "not the smallest letter or stroke shall pass away from the Law, until all is accomplished" (Matthew 5:18). Beyond any question, Jesus Christ validates the Scripture.

Critics have retaliated, "How do we know that Jesus actually said the words that are in the Bible?" Well, the Hebrew custom at that time was that you never wrote down anything as true unless you had heard it with your own ears and had two eyewitnesses for corroboration. The historical evidence is that the Bible contains the actual words of Jesus.

So critics retaliate one more time. They say Jesus was mistaken when He said, "I and the Father are One" (John 10:30). Can an infallible God make a mistake? Can a holy God deceive? The attack on the authenticity of Jesus' words is really a guise for the belief that He is not who He says He is, a challenge to the fact that He was actually resurrected from the dead.

It's an attack that has gone on for nearly 2,000 years. Indeed, it began in the first century, for that is why the Apostle Paul wrote to the church at Corinth,

> If Christ has not been raised, your faith is worthless; you are still in your sins. Then those also who have fallen asleep in Christ

have perished. If we have hoped in Christ in this life only, we are of all men most to be pitied (1 Corinthians 15:17-19).

But if Jesus Christ was resurrected in fulfillment of the Scripture, He is who He says He is and has the authority to say that the Bible *is* the Word of God.

Oddly enough, what ultimately persuaded me of the Bible's truth was my own experience in the Watergate scandal. It was March 21, 1973, when John Dean walked into President Nixon's office and said, "Mr. President, there is a cancer growing on your presidency." And that was the day he laid out everything about the Watergate cover-up to Mr. Nixon. That's the first time we really knew it was a criminal conspiracy that could involve the White House. There was talk of perjury, obstruction of justice — the type of things that give grown men sweaty palms. It was on April 8, 1973, as John Dean confessed in his memoirs, that he went to the prosecutor to turn himself in and "to save his own skin." He would testify against the President in exchange for immunity from prosecution.

And at that point the conspiracy was gone.

Mr. Nixon didn't know it at the time, but he was finished. Jeb Magruder went to the prosecutor next; then a half-dozen other people. I took a lie detector test to show I knew nothing about the Watergate break-in. My lawyers released it to the *New York Times.* We were all scrambling to save our own skins. The Watergate cover-up, the really criminal part, lasted less than three weeks.

Put yourself in our shoes. There we were, ten or eleven of the most powerful men in the world, the colleagues of the President of the United States. We could press a button and have a jet waiting for us at Andrews Air Force Base. We could order government agencies around, deal with heads of nations. We had all this power at our fingertips, but when threatened with jail and political embarrassment, we couldn't contain a lie for even three weeks.

Now contrast Watergate with the apostles' testimony about the Resurrection. For forty years those men, who were powerless — without money, armies, or resources — proclaimed throughout Palestine and the Roman Empire that Jesus had been bodily raised from the dead. Every one of them went to jail and was persecuted. All but one died a martyr's death.

They could never have maintained their story that was so offensive to the powerful of their day unless it were true and they had seen the risen Christ. The Apostle Peter would have been just like John Dean. There would have been a deathbed confession, a smoking-gun tape, something. But the evidence is overwhelming that not once in those forty years did any of the apostles renounce Jesus. They had seen Him!

The evidence for the resurrection of Jesus Christ is more powerful than anything else we believe. By His resurrection Jesus proved He is who He says He is. Be confident in this truth. Stand on the Holy Word of God. Don't sell the world a false bill of goods. Preach the Word. Defend the faith. Live the faith.

Just a Social Club?

The third error the world makes concerning the church is seeing us as something like a Sunday morning Rotary Club, a place you join, visit to be inspired, and stay as long as you feel like staying. When people tell me, "That was a very inspiring message," I always feel disappointed because I don't want to entertain. I want to bring the truth. And the truth is convicting.

The Apostle Paul, writing to Timothy, described the church as the "pillar and support of the truth" (1 Timothy 3:15). In this context he isn't using *truth* to refer to something being factual, as in this truth: I sit at a desk that is made of wood. No, Paul is referring to *truth* in the sense that Jesus used the word when he said, "I am the truth" (John 14:6). We Christians — the church — take our stand on this revealed, propositional truth.

When he was gasping for breath, near death, Francis Schaeffer told me that the crisis we face is one of truth. "The issue is truth," he often said, "and there'll be nothing but an echo of truth left before the end of this century."

Increasingly in this age, holding this truth will make you the subject of scorn and ridicule. Increasingly Christians will be tempted to say, "I'll just edge over here a bit to be a little more in tune with the values of the society"; they'll want to join the "church as social club."

If we can't call people to be disciples and teach them to pray, to study, to live holy lives as witnesses for Jesus Christ, we have no business being a church. We might as well shut the doors and close down.

It's high time the church became bold in its witness; we have too long watered down our message for fear of offending people. The Gospel minces no words: To be a Christian is to be a member of a holy nation, the central covenant of which is that a holy God has chosen to come and live in our midst, a God who commands, "You shall be holy, for I am holy" (1 Peter 1:16). We must be a holy people, not just pious in the way we live our lives but holy in the sense that we fight for God's standards of justice and righteousness in society.

It does not matter so much what we do in this success-oriented world in which we live as what a sovereign God chooses to do through us. What really matters is not our achievements, but our right relationship with the living Lord and our willingness to live obedient Christian lives so that Christ can work through us, to be the people of hope in a world of despair. That's what Jesus means when He says, "He who has lost his life for My sake shall find it" (Matthew 10:39). The great paradox of the Christian life is that God will use you in ways you least expect. What He wants is for you to obey Him, to do as He commands.

Wherever I go, I ask people, "What is the greatest commandment of the Christian life?"

And almost every believer answers, "To love the Lord your God with all your heart, mind, and soul."

Then I follow up by asking, "What do you mean by 'love the Lord'?"

It's marvelous the kinds of answers you get when you ask that question. People generally reply, "I feel a wonderful feeling toward Him," or, "I worship Him." Yet Jesus gives us the answer in the simplest possible terms. He says, "If you love Me, you will keep My commandments" (John 14:15).

Obedience is the beginning of the Christian life; obedience is essential to truly living as a Christian. But on every side today we are beset by temptations that carry us away from God. We live in the most materialistic, egocentric time in American history. It's hard to be obedient to Christ in our pressure-packed society. It's tough to be an obedient Christian when our culture worships a false god of success. The world says, "Do your own thing"; the Gospel says, "Bear one another's burdens, and thus fulfill the Law of Christ" (Galatians 6:2). The world says, "Look out for number one"; the Gospel says to "lay down our lives for the brethren" (1 John 3:16) and to "love your neighbor as yourself" (Mark 12:31). It takes courage to be obedient, courage found only in total dependence on the Holy Spirit.

We Cannot Fail!

There isn't any hope in our society except the hope that comes from the people of God living righteously in our land. There is no ultimate hope through government or human institutions. Our brightest and best leaders are concerned with the question, "How shall we be governed?" But in the Book of Ezekiel the Jews asked: "How shall we live?" It doesn't matter who governs if society has no spiritual element to guide it.

I have seen this truth most powerfully in the area in which I've been called to spend my life: bringing Christ's healing to our crime crisis. Criminologist James Q. Wilson, among others, has tried to identify the root cause of this epidemic of violence. When he began his inquiry, he was certain that he would discover that in the great period of industrial revolution in the latter half of the nineteenth century there was a tremendous increase in crime. But, to his astonishment, he discovered a decrease. And then he looked at the years of the Great Depression. Again, there was a significant decrease in crime. Frustrated by these findings, which upset all our preconceived notions, Wilson decided to search for a single factor to correlate. The factor he found was religious faith.

When crime should have been rising in the late 1800s because of rapid urbanization, industralization, and economic dislocation, Victorian morality was sweeping across America. It was a time of intense spirituality. It was not until the conscious rejection of Victorian morality during the Roaring Twenties that crime went up. This was the era when Sigmund Freud's views were coming into vogue among "thinking" Americans: people weren't evil, just misguided or mistreated, or they required better environments. Sin was regarded as a lot of religious claptrap.

The crime rate did not decline again until the Great Depression, a time of people band-

ing together in the face of crisis. Wilson concluded, therefore, that crime was in large part
caused by a breakdown of morality. Since 1965
the violent-crime rate has steadily risen. In the
same period, religious faith has waned. We
have told people there are no absolutes and
that they are not responsible for their own be-
havior. They are simply victims of a system
that isn't working anymore, and they don't
have to worry about it because the government
is going to fix it for them. Well, the secular
utopia is in reality the nightmare we see as we
walk through the dark, rotten holes we call
prisons all across America.

In this context, it always amazes me when I
listen to politicians say, "We are going to win
the war on drugs by building prisons, appoint-
ing more judges, and putting more police on
the beat. I remember when President Bush
announced the "War on Drugs."

Having spent seven months in prison, there
wasn't one night that I did not smell marijuana
burning. If you can get marijuana into a prison,
with watchtowers, inspections, and prison
guards, you can get it into a country. You can
send the U.S. Marines to Colombia to burn all
the fields, seal all the borders, and build all

the prisons you want, but you won't stop drug use in this country because it isn't a problem of supply; it is a problem of demand. When there is no greater value in the lives of so many people than simply fulfilling individual desires and gratifications, then crime and drug use become inevitable. The soaring violent-crime rate is powerful testimony to the failure of the city of man, deprived of the moral influence of the City of God.

Sometimes we Christians think our ultimate power is in the ballot box, when our power is really in the cross of Jesus Christ. Realizing this, we must also realize the importance of our role as believers—faithfully to obey the holy commandments of God. We cannot allow the newspapers to define the church's role. Nor television. Nor the politicians. Man may fail, but the church—God's chosen instrument—cannot fail.

Speaking to His disciple Peter, Jesus spoke of the church of Christ: "The gates of hell shall not prevail against it" (Matthew 16:18, KJV). They never have and they never will.

Late in the last century there was a great Methodist church planter named C.C. McKay who traveled around the country planting one new church a day. While in Oregon one day, he read a newspaper report of a speech given to the Free Thinkers Society by noted lawyer and orator Robert Ingersoll. In the report Ingersoll, an atheist, was quoted as saying that the church was dying. C.C. McKay got off the train, went to the telegraph office, and cabled the following message to Robert Ingersoll:

Dear Bob,

In the Methodist church we are starting one new congregation a day. And now because of what you said, we propose to make it two.

C.C. McKay

P.S. All hail the power of Jesus' name.

The telegram prompted a series of debates between McKay and Ingersoll—most of them won by McKay—as well as a wonderful folk hymn, sung in Methodist churches all across the land.

But the most wonderful footnote of the story didn't happen until years later. In 1941 Ingersoll's grandson, Robert Ingersoll III, walked into a church in Chicago, heard the Gospel, believed, was baptized, and became a member of that congregation. So did Robert Ingersoll IV a few days afterward.

All hail the power of Jesus' name! The church is alive!

CHAPTER THREE

Presenting Belief in an Age of Unbelief

F or more than thirty years each technological advance and expansion of government power was measured against the vision of George Orwell's extraordinary novel *1984.*

Now, in retrospect, the judgment of most commentators has been nearly unanimous: Orwell, sick and disillusioned with the vain promise of Socialist utopia, was overly pessimistic. He underestimated the strength of the West economically and politically, failed to reckon with the human spirit, and as a struggling agnostic, could not anticipate the work of a sovereign God in history. There has been no "Big Brother" or "Newspeak" (at least not in the obvious form Orwell pictured), no telescreens or thought control. We have escaped those dire predictions — so far. But have we really?

There is, I believe, a profound insight buried in Orwell's exaggerated satire. It is captured in this reflection of Winston Smith's: "It struck him [Orwell] that the truly characteristic thing about modern life was not its cruelty and insecurity but simply its barrenness, its dinginess, its listlessness." Smith continues, saying that in such a milieu, "Orthodoxy means not thinking, not needing to think; orthodoxy is unconsciousness."

The Sin of Our Times

If we are honest, it would be difficult to find a more accurate characterization of our times. And if we are honest, we are forced to admit that what only a tyrannical Big Brother could accomplish in Orwell's *1984*, our self-indulgent Western society has very nearly managed to do to itself today. Of course, our seduction has been more subtle and therefore far more insidious — through the influences of mass media and advertising, the relentless pursuit of hedonism, and the unthinking, uncritical acceptance of prevailing and declining moral and educational values.

We have, to an alarming degree, become victims of our own mindless conformity — self-absorbed, indifferent, empty of heart, the "hollow men" that T.S. Eliot wrote about in the early part of the century. Yes, orthodoxy has become unconsciousness; nihilism is the spirit of this spiritless age.

A tragic example of this was the death of David Kennedy, the fourth son of the late Senator Robert Kennedy. Kennedy, twenty-eight, was found dead in a Palm Beach, Florida hotel room, apparently the victim of a drug overdose.

Referring to David's struggle with drugs, a friend reported to *The Washington Post,* "In David's case, there was nothing to connect to in life. Even free of the drug influence, there was a deep, overpowering sense of nihilism in his personality. No person, no job, no hobby could give him something to plug into."

Dorothy Sayers, the astute contemporary of C.S. Lewis, said the sin of our times is the sin that believes in nothing, cares for nothing, seeks to know nothing, interferes with nothing, enjoys nothing, hates nothing, finds purpose in nothing, lives for nothing, and remains alive because there is nothing for which it will die.

When researcher George Barna asked Americans if they believed there was any such thing as absolute truth, 66 percent said no. When he posed the same question to conservative evangelical Christians, 53 percent said they didn't believe in absolute truth. Barna's research also showed that 44 percent of the baby-boomers say there's no cause that would lead them to fight and die for their country. Well, without the underpinnings of *truth*, what is there — beyond *self* — to live or die for?

Totalitarianism is not the conquering tyrant, enslaving us to the state; it is nihilism. We have yielded to the insidious enslavement of self-gratification. The villain, in short, is us, even those who call themselves Christians.

Too extreme a view, you say? Consider just these few manifestations:

● In the name of the "right" of a woman to

control her own body, 28 million unborn children have been murdered in America since 1973, when abortion was legalized. Who, I might ask, has inflicted a more widespread tyranny—Hitler, a maniacal dictator, or an uncaring, indifferent society? Sure, a few "religious fanatics" rant and rave, but most people are unmoved. Orthodoxy has become unconsciousness.

● As a society, we have believed Socrates, that sin is the result of ignorance, and Hegel, that man is evolving through increasing knowledge to superior moral levels. And so we've done away with any sense of individual responsibility.

What delusions! In this, the most educated and advanced society the world has ever known, we have a 50 percent divorce rate, soaring violent-crime rates, and widespread child abuse and neglect. . . . A valueless culture breeds the most awful tyranny.

● As a nation we have been blessed with unprecedented material abundance; but what it has produced is a boredom so pervasive that drug use is epidemic. A few years back I was talking with an extremely successful businessman, a great entrepreneur whose name you would immediately know. He told me excitedly that he had discovered a great untapped potential business: drug and alcohol rehabilitation. "It's the fastest growth industry in America, with surefire profits," he told me. So dramatic has been the recent increase in drug and alcohol addiction that our facilities are completely incapable of handling the casualties.

The obsessive egocentricity of secular culture today—Scott Peck calls it "narcissism" in his book *People of the Lie*—creates a special tyranny of its own. Like the young woman cited in a *Psychology Today* magazine article, her nerves shot from too many all-night parties, her life an endless round of pot, booze, and sex. When asked by a therapist, "Why don't you stop?" her startled reply was, "You mean I really don't have to do what I want to do?"

Who is the tyrant in our hedonistic society? Not Big Brother. Us.

Francis Schaeffer used to say that modern man has both feet planted firmly in midair.

The Church in Trouble

But the most frightening fact of our world today is that the church of Jesus Christ is in almost as much trouble as the culture. Unthinkingly, we have almost completely bought into the counterfeit secular value system. In fact, we can one-up it, since God is on our side. Unfortunately, this skewed Gospel and cheap grace are what prevent the church from making any real impact for Christ.

Many Christians attribute our impotence to the fact that we are being overrun by the culture, victimized by the media; that the reason we can't get our message across to the secular world is because we are thwarted by those who control the all-powerful tube.

And powerful it is. A study conducted by the *Detroit Free Press* showed that adults as well as children, when cut off from TV, suffer symptoms similar to drug withdrawal. Significantly, 120 households were offered $500 each to participate in the study, giving up thirty days of television. Only 27 accepted.

Christian philosopher Soren Kierkegaard was uncannily prophetic when more than a century ago he wrote,

Suppose someone invented an instrument, a convenient little talking tube, which could be heard over the whole land. I wonder if the police would forbid it fearing that the whole country would become mentally deranged if it were used.

Those who can control the tube or other forms of media wield tremendous power. For instance, when I speak to the media about my conversion, I *always* deliberately say, "I accepted Jesus Christ"; but reporters will invariably translate that into my "religious conversion," or "conversion to Christianity," or even "born again," now that the term has been so secularized as to be harmless. How the world fears the person of Jesus Christ! Christianity? Fine. It preaches peace. But introduce a risen Lord and that arouses fierce antagonism.

One major American daily, in fact, refuses to use the word "Christ" when speaking about Jesus. To do so would be to make an editorial judgment—that Jesus was the Messiah.

But there is another side. When once I was with the president of one of the television networks, I chided him for not putting more wholesome family programming on prime-time television. And since Gallup polls show that one third of all Americans claim to be born again, I told him he was missing a good market by not airing more shows with Christian values.

"Oh," he replied, "You mean like *Chariots of Fire?*"

"Yes," I exclaimed. "I've seen it ten times. I think it's one of the most powerful penetrations of the Gospel into the arts in this generation."

"Well," he said, "CBS ran *Chariots of Fire* as its Sunday Night Movie some months ago. That same night NBC had *On Golden Pond* and ABC had *My Mother's Secret Life* — a soap opera about a mother who was hiding her past as a prostitute. Let me tell you the ratings. *On Golden Pond* was number one, with 25.2 percent of all TV sets in America tuned in. *My Mother's Secret Life* drew a rating of 25.1 percent. Way in the distance, losing its shirt was CBS with *Chariots of Fire* — 11.8 percent. Of the sixty-five shows rated that week 'Dallas' was number one, *Chariots of Fire* number fifty-seven."

Then he looked at me smugly and asked, "So where, Mr. Colson, are your 50 million born-again Christians?" I had no answer. Where were we? Where are we?

You see, in *1984* — the novel, that is — the instrument by which Big Brother controlled people was the telescreen. He saw everything; if they looked back into the telescreen they saw Big Brother. But when *we* look into the television set we see something much more terrifying than the image of Big Brother. We see ourselves. Television is but a mirror reflection. Orthodoxy has become unconsciousness.

Alexander Solzhenitsyn, the Nobel laureate whom I consider one of the greatest prophetic voices of God today, captured the dilemma of our times brilliantly in his speech accepting the Templeton Prize for the Advancement of Religion. He recalled during his childhood in Russia that when great disasters came, people would respond, "Men have forgotten God. That's why all this has happened." And in his survey of twentieth-century Western culture, Solzhenitsyn could find nothing better to describe what has happened than that pithy Russian proverb, "Men have forgotten God."

The great drama of our day is deeper than totalitarianism versus democracy or East versus West. The real struggle is belief versus unbelief.

Is Carl Sagan's creed, which is taught in our schools, correct — that "the Cosmos is all there is or ever will be" — or is there a sovereign God who manifests Himself in His Word and in the person of Jesus Christ, the same yesterday, to-day, and forever? That's the great battle—and it's uphill.

The Challenge of Change

So the great question for us as evangelical Christians charged with making disciples of all nations, is how to fulfill our biblical commission in such a time as this, bringing meaning to a culture wallowing in meaninglessness.

How *do* we present a message of belief in an age of unbelief? Charting our course is made all the more challenging when we recognize that the very nature of evangelicalism, evangelism included, as we've known it is in a time of transition, making some dramatic changes inevitable.

Consider just these four factors of change:

The first is leadership. Over the past four de-cades, one man, Billy Graham, has been singular-ly used of God—quite possibly as the greatest evangelist of all time. I hope Billy will continue preaching for a long, long time. John Wesley did until he was eighty-seven. But we evangelicals who have relied so heavily on him must recog-nize that the day will come when he cannot.

That day will, I believe, also mark the end of the era of stadium mass evangelism—at least in the United States. Billy's unique charisma always generates a sense of expectancy and excitement, but for anyone else, and for almost any other purpose, with each passing year it becomes more difficult to bring thousands into stadiums. There are a host of sociological reasons: crime in urban areas, television, growing public apathy, lack of effective organization, to mention but a few.

In my opinion, when the mantle of leadership is passed, it will fall not to any one individual, but to hundreds, perhaps thousands. One of the most thrilling moments of my Christian life was to see nearly 5,000 evangelists from all over the world in Amsterdam for Billy's first conference for itinerant evangelists in 1983. It is impossible for me to describe the excitement in that auditorium. Men and women from every nation sat furiously taking notes as Billy and others shared their most intimate experiences as evangelists and coached them on how to preach, how to prepare sermons, how to discern the needs of their audience. I hope Billy will do much more of this in the years ahead, and that through this remarkable man God will continue to raise up thousands of disciples to plant the Gospel in every corner of the earth. But we must recognize that evangelism leadership will be diffused — and spread around the world.

The second is the changing nature of the media. As the extraordinary technological breakthroughs of recent years — instant communications, home satellite receivers, and the like — have dramatically changed American habits, so have they begun to change the character of the American evangelist. Modern technology permitted the remarkable growth of Christian television and created new Christian folk heroes almost overnight. So great was the hunger of the evangelical viewer to be affirmed in his own beliefs that funds poured in.

But the honeymoon was short-lived, for many reasons, one being that television, by its very nature, must provide ever-increasing thrills to hold its audience; otherwise its viewers just switch channels. And to catch the attention of viewers used to thirty-second commercials, it has to reduce the Gospel message to simple slogans.

As the novelty of Christian TV wore off, a winnowing process began. TV evangelists tell me that even in good markets it is difficult to maintain their needed financial support. As TV evangelists are "forced" to plead for funds to remain on the air, airtime for the real message grows less and less.

I hasten to add, however, that quality programming with theological integrity will prosper. Witness the incredible growth of Jim Dobson's outstanding radio series, just to mention one of many examples.

Third, the great charismatic explosion, which began several decades ago, may be tapering off. Traditional evangelicals, by the way, owe much to the charismatic movement for bringing back to the church a sense of the supernatural, of worship, of adoration. But like all movements that begin with great spontaneity, this too is becoming institutionalized and large numbers of charismatics are settling into the mainstream of the church.

Fourth, the process of "privatization," as Os Guinness calls it, sadly will intensify as society becomes more impersonal and individuals feel more alienated. People will, I fear, continue to compartmentalize their lives including their religious experience. Ask a Christian layperson his ministry and he will inevitably respond, "Gideons on

Thursday night," or "Prison Fellowship on Monday night," or, "Sunday School." The process of privatization destroys our understanding of ministry that is twenty-four hours a day, being Christ's person wherever we are, in business, the home, the country club, or the ghetto.

Jay Kesler, president of Taylor University, says the church today is like a pro football game: 100,000 people sitting in the stands watching 22 men on the field beating themselves to a pulp. True Christianity is not a spectator sport; it is not to be sat out in church pews; it is to be lived out in the world so that "the blessings of God might show forth in every area of life" as the great Puritan pastor Cotton Mather put it.

These developments should cause us thoughtfully and prayerfully to examine our strategy for evangelism for the balance of this century. In this spirit, let me suggest five areas of challenge and opportunity.

Witness As a Way of Life

First, authentic evangelism must involve the totality of life. Jesus said, "You *shall* be My witnesses," but a lot of Christians have taken that commandment to mean that we are *to* witness. So we have reduced evangelism to verbal formulas, neat, easy-step plans; just utter these simple phrases and you'll be part of the club.

And some people seem to think that the simpler we can communicate the Gospel, the more people we can recruit. Maybe so, but the question is "recruit them for what?" Millard Fuller of Habitat for Humanity tells the story of his experience in Zaire, where Christians had trained parrots to say, "I love Jesus." Not unfairly, I think, Fuller likens many who sit in pews every Sunday morning, mindlessly chanting their creeds, to those parrots.

Packaging the Gospel into tidy packages has some serious dangers. For one thing, it tends to cheapen the message. When we tell the world that all there is to becoming a Christian is a simple prayer—and thereafter God will shower blessings upon them—we are selling the world a false bill of goods. We will pay for it—if not from the angry disillusioned millions to whom we sell our false message, then surely on Judgment Day. Then too we can easily fall into the snare of turning evangelism into a big game hunt—keeping score and measuring success by the fame and power of our convert trophies.

This is why it is so important to focus on Jesus' command that we *be* witnesses. Jesus means, I believe, that evangelism is to involve the totality of our lives. Everything about our lifestyle counts — how we spend our money, how we treat our children, our business ethics, our political values, our domestic relations, and on and on. (And this means far more than being faithful in church every Sunday morning or not smoking, drinking, using foul language, or associating with those who do.)

Christians are supposed to be humble, yet we can get caught up in our own importance and power. During a press conference at a Christian broadcasters' convention, a reporter from a prominent national daily challenged me, "I don't know what all this born-again business means, but I have been at this convention two days, and everywhere I go the people I interview seem to think they have all the answers. As a matter of fact, the bigger the exhibit, the more arrogant the individual. Aren't born-again Christians supposed to be loving?"

I defended my brethren, pointing out that

most of them enter the ministry for all the best reasons, but that we Christians are not immune to the seduction of power. But I had to bite my lip because I know exactly what that reporter was talking about—and so do you.

As we present the Gospel to an unbelieving world we need to hold before us the words of Paul: "Let this mind be in you, which was also in Christ Jesus." Though He was God, He "made Himself of no reputation, and took upon Him the form of a servant" (Philippians 2:5, 7, KJV).

When I came to Christ I realized that my great sin had been pride. But those words— "let this mind be in you"—ring in my ears constantly. God does not let me forget them and my utter dependency on Him for grace to reach out to others in His name.

How we need to be reminded of the oft-quoted adage that "evangelism is like one beggar showing another beggar where he found bread."

Joseph Bayly's book *The Gospel Blimp* should be mandatory reading for evangelicals. While we are creating sophisticated organizations and employing the latest technology to win the world to Christ, let us not forget that our neighbors judge Jesus Christ by what they see in us.

Discipling Believers

Second, evangelism demands serious discipleship. Our task is not simply to get people to recite certain prayers so we can move on to more fertile fields. We are to help lead them to Christ and then teach them spiritual disciplines and truths so that they truly can become disciples — followers of Christ, and in time, teachers themselves. One-on-one ministries like The Navigators will, I believe, become increasingly strategic in the decades ahead.

When I asked Christ into my life, I had never heard of evangelical Christianity. I didn't know the jargon or formulas of the evangelical subculture. If there hadn't been someone to take me by the hand and walk me through the Scriptures, help me to pray, help me to feel comfortable with others, I really wonder where I would be today. Doug Coe discipled me constantly. Harold Hughes, my one-time political enemy, loved me even when most people in my own political party turned their backs on me. Al Quie, then a congressman, offered to go to prison for me. Fred Rhodes took early retirement from government to help me start Prison Fellowship. And down through the years there have been men like Carl Henry, Richard Lovelace, R.C. Sproul, Dick Halverson, and others who have given so much of themselves to teach me. Whatever growth I have experienced as a Christian has been in large measure due to the sacrificial commitment of others who were willing to invest themselves in me.

And this kind of evangelism cannot be deterred. Mass evangelism through television could be eliminated tomorrow. Funds could dry up; government policies could change; so could media ownership; we could be subjected to oppression in this country that would deny the free proclamation of the Gospel.

But there is no power than can ever stop one-on-one discipleship. Across the country Prison Fellowship has trained a band of dedicated men and women who mentor Christian prisoners facing the tough transition back to the outside world. Clair VanZeelt of Chicago demonstrates the commitment of some of these volunteers. Even before being trained—on his very first trip inside Cook County Jail—Clair met inmate Jimmy. Handing Jimmy a printed Bible study lesson, Clair said, "I'll be back next week and give you another one."

When Clair returned, Jimmy had been transferred to another, tougher facility. Though it took Clair two weeks to cut through red tape, he found Jimmy and delivered a second lesson. When Clair returned a third time, Jimmy was overwhelmed. "You're probably the best friend I've ever had," he told Clair, who was himself amazed. "I had spent maybe a total of one hour with him," Clair says. "But his family and society had rejected him. Right then I came to appreciate what it means to express love." That was thirteen years ago, and now dozens of ex-prisoners know that Clair—"Dad"—is on the other end of the phone line, standing by with a steady hand and a word of encouragement grounded in the Word of God.

It is reported that when the missionaries left China and the Communists took over, the most awful persecution of the church, then estimated at more than 1 million believers, began. Surely, after thirty years of brutal, ruthless persecution, the church would be obliterated; instead, according to many reports, there are today more than 30 million Christians in China.

Joseph Stalin once mockingly dismissed the church's influence, asking how many divisions the Pope had. What would he say now when the church has survived and proved more powerful than the political party he ruled with an iron fist?

Penetrating the Culture

Third, for effective evangelism we must penetrate the mainstream of thought in secular culture.

Since only 8 percent of secular reporters regularly attend church, it is not surprising that most fail to discern spiritual matters. Nicaragua is a clear example. The Pope stood alone on a platform to conduct mass while Sandinista officials held back the huge, friendly crowd, took over the front-row seats, and for the benefit of the grinding TV cameras, shook their fists and screamed at the Pope.

Each time they did so, the Pope lifted his crucifix over his head. A remarkable linguist, he conducted mass in the language of the Miskito Indians, thousands of whom the Sandinistas had ruthlessly murdered. Symbolically he conveyed the powerful truth: God offers grace to the people you killed. The crowd cheered, while the protestors howled with rage at the Pope's open defiance.

It was a classic confrontation, reminding me of what historian Will Durant called the greatest drama of history—when Christ met Caesar in the arena—and Christ won. For without doubt, that unforgettable night in Managua, Christ won.

But what did American newsmen on the scene report of that classic confrontation? What did they see and hear? The Pope was inept and confused, they said, speaking in a language the crowd couldn't understand. And he failed to bring peace or healing to that troubled country. He berated Marxist priests and further divided his church.

Of course he did—and deliberately. He also indicted the Sandinistas for their massacres and their politicization of the church. He held up the indestructible truth of Christ against their shouted insults. But he did not achieve overnight reform; so the media labeled as "failure" what was in reality a truly heroic moment for Christians.

Subliminally, a nuance and a word at a time, the non-Christian perspective inexorably gains ground. If C.S. Lewis were alive today he might write of Screwtape's sad fate: Alas, he is among the unemployed; things are going quite nicely without his having to lift a finger.

To invade the secular mainstream means that Christian writers and others with creative talents must compete in the secular media. We need to infiltrate the newsrooms of *The Washington Post* and the *New York Times*, of CBS, ABC, and NBC.

We need to frame the issues in a Christian worldview. Some years ago two Los Angeles doctors were accused of murder. They had removed the life support apparatus from a comatose man whose condition they diagnosed irreversible. First went the respirator; he began to breathe on his own. Then the doctors ceased intravenous feeding. Nine days later the man died—of starvation. NBC's anchorman pegged the story with the following: "The question of when to pull the plug may be about to get a thorough hearing in a Los Angeles courtroom."

When to pull the plug? What about *if?* The treatment of a dying man is full of ethical dilemmas. But are they all to be framed in terms of *when* to pull the plug? Have we already concluded that we must pull it?

The anchorman's words suggest that the decision is merely complex, not agonizing. A cost-benefit analysis, which could be done on a computer, might resolve the moral questions. Convenience and productivity and overall cost determine who lives and who dies.

This is a scenario borrowed from the pages of Alexander Solzhenitsyn's *Cancer Ward.* In the Soviet Union, in a society free from moral impediments, that is how decisions were made.

We Christians tend to hurl invectives at the "satanic enemy" and claim it's all part of a sinister conspiracy. I overreacted in the same way during my White House days when I believed the media distorted their coverage of Mr. Nixon to suit their own biases. But the fact is that secular journalists do not choose their words as part of some conscious plot to destroy Christian values. No, it's worse than that: The choice is unconscious, simply reflecting the worldview of the writer. The word "when" is what most naturally came to mind; to a Christian, the word "if" would be natural.

We need Christian influence in the media and in the arts and in music so that God's truth becomes evident in every walk of life.

In that same vein, Christian scholars and thinkers need to do battle with secular intellects. I realize that many Christians believe that reason and faith are incompatible. But that is nonsense. Augustine said, "Believe that you may understand, understand that you may believe."

Let's face it, friends, if we fail to articulate the reasoned defense of our faith, all of our witnessing, plans of salvation, and evangelistic efforts will be for naught. Secularization of Western culture is undermining the presuppositions absolutely essential for effective evangelization. In a society that has lost a common belief in moral absolutes, relativism reigns — thus the Bible is just another book and Jesus simply another superior teacher.

Abraham Kuyper was a great Dutch theologian in the early part of this century. Kuyper argued that if Christians are going to be strong enough to stand against the philosophy of secularism, they must articulate a philosophy that is just as comprehensive as secularism. Christianity must be an all-embracing system of thought that gives us a perspective from which to view every part of life: family, church, work, politics, science, art, and culture.

In short, Christianity must be a worldview: a view of the entire world, an intellectual grid through which we can interpret everything we see or read or do. God created the world, and everything in the world relates to Him.

Kuyper didn't just talk about Christianity as a worldview. He acted on it. He worked vigorously to influence public life in the Netherlands on the basis of Christian truth. He founded a Christian university, published a newspaper, wrote daily editorials, and was eventually elected prime minister. Kuyper's social and educational reforms continue to benefit Holland today.

When the Apostle Paul preached in Athens — a culture that did not know the Scriptures — he was not afraid to introduce the Gospel in terms they would understand. He quoted Greek poetry. On Mars Hill he saw a monument to "the unknown god." Seeing that they acknowledged that a deity might exist whom they didn't know, Paul jumped at the opportunity. He saw a jumping-off point from which he could proclaim the Good News of Christ. He was willing to engage the Greek mind before he presented the Gospel.

There's a clear parallel here. We no longer live in Jerusalem. Our country is an "Athens"—unfamiliar with and hostile to our God. We cannot compromise the message, but we've got to find ways to present what we believe in a way they can understand it.

Much of our Christianity today is, sadly, entertainment for the faithful. We talk in our own language to likeminded friends, and the world is content to let us put on our own show, as long as we don't bother anyone.

But we are meant to bother the world—bother it by presenting a message that convicts people of their sin, which offers an alternative to the hollowness and nihilism of secular life.

To invade the secular mainstream—on their turf—requires great creativity and boldness. It means aggressively reaching out and battling for the hearts and minds of our neighbors.

But we can do it. That's why I was so thrilled with the advertising campaign sponsored by the Arthur S. DeMoss Foundation offering *Power for Living*, a little booklet that magnificently presented the Gospel message. It was offered over secular television and in full-page ads in the *Wall Street Journal*, the

Washington Post, and other publications. More than 7 millon people responded for information about the Gospel: tens of thousands have come to Christ through that magnificent outreach.

And we can do it on a more personal level, also. Just before a governor's prayer breakfast where I was to speak, the chairman asked me not to mention the name of Jesus Christ because there were Jews in the audience. You know what to do with advice like that—and that's what I did. The first people to thank me afterward were Jewish. Don't ever water down your message for anyone.

We need to stop talking to ourselves and speak instead to the secular world. There is real hunger out there. John Wesley said the "way to a man's heart is through his mind," so we need to be giving quality Christian literature to our non-Christian neighbors. My own Christian life began because a Christian friend handed me *Mere Christianity.* Let's lead people to the real meat: the great classics by and about Augustine, Jonathan Edwards, John Calvin, Charles Spurgeon, Dietrich Bonhoeffer, C.S. Lewis or contemporaries like Francis Schaeffer, J.I. Packer, Malcolm Muggeridge, Carl Henry, and others of their caliber.

Strengthening the Role of the Church

Fourth, the role of the church in evangelism must be strengthened. We evangelicals have had a sinfully, shamefully casual disregard for that institution for which our Lord shed His own blood. He gave Himself up for the body of Christ — the church — that the church would be the presence of God in the world, that people would see the kingdom-of-God-to-come in the people of God.

In our well-intentioned zeal to win the whole world for Christ, we have tended to concentrate on grand crusades and in the process we often diminish the responsibility of the local church. This is one of the reasons that many churches have become nothing more than Sunday morning civic clubs, places where people go for their one-hour-a-week inspirational fix.

We have allowed ourselves to drift a long way from the biblical vision of the church. Listen to how Aristides described the early church to Hadrian the Roman Emperor:

They love one another, they never fail to help widows, they save orphans from those who would hurt them. If they have something they give freely to the man who has nothing. If they see a stranger they take him home, and are happy as though he were a real brother. They don't consider themselves brothers in the usual sense, but brothers instead through the Spirit, in God.

That is evangelism, when people *see* God's power lived as a new order, their values in sharp contrast to the ways of the world. That's making the "invisible kingdom visible," as John Calvin puts it.

The success of evangelism in the next decade, I am convinced, will be in direct proportion to the strength of the local church. But because we have failed to make the church all that it is supposed to be, the culture doesn't expect much from it.

When I was in New York recently, a cab driver asked me what I do for a living.

"I'm a minister," I answered, trying to explain my writing and speaking activities in a word he would understand—not that I am an ordained clergyman.

"Oho," the cabbie said. "So you're here to get money."

119

It wasn't a question; it was a statement: If you're a minister, *that's* what you're after. Money.

The cabbie launched into a well-worn diatribe against Christians. "A bunch of hypocrites," he said. And he clinched his case with the Jimmy Swaggart scandal.

Frankly, it was hard to respond. I had no defense. The Jimmy Swaggart case has brought disgrace on the entire evangelical world. One person falls, and we're all painted with the same brush.

To its credit, the Assemblies of God did its best to discipline Jimmy Swaggart after his first offense, when he was caught with a prostitute. The denomination ordered him to step down from the pulpit and undergo counseling.

But Swaggart refused. Even when the denomination revoked his license to preach, he continued his ministry.

And people continued to support him.

Then Swaggart dishonored the church a second time — caught with another prostitute. This time, he was even less repentant. He told his congregation, "The Lord told me it's flat none of your business."

The lesson here is this: When a believer is

disciplined by his church, *and refuses to comply,* then the scriptural principle is to cast him out of the congregation.

The policy is described in Matthew 18: If a believer rejects the discipline of the church and continues in sin, expel him. And Paul's letter to the Corinthians explains why.

The purpose is not to be mean or vengeful. It's to impress upon the sinner the seriousness of his sin, with the hope of bringing him to repentance. *And* it's to maintain the integrity of the church before a watching world.

When the Assemblies of God church disciplined Jimmy Swaggart, the rest of the Christian world should have refused to tune in to Swaggart's program anymore or send him money.

But many people chose to follow a charismatic TV preacher instead of the church. They continued to listen to Swaggart and give him financial support.

Swaggart himself is ultimately responsible for his second offense, of course. But so are the Christians who enabled him to continue in ministry after he had defied the discipline of his church. Is it any wonder the world laughs at our evangelistic efforts?

Demonstrating the Gospel

Fifth, evangelism is more than proclamation; it is demonstration. We live in an age of deep skepticism. Most surveys reveal that people do not believe what they see and hear through the media. (Perhaps we can be grateful for that.) Public respect for institutions and professions has steadily declined. Ministers do a little better in public opinion polls than politicians, but that is not saying much.

PF's *Jubilee* newsletter recently ran a story of ex-prisoner Herbie Harris. One paragraph in his story caught my attention. For eighteen months Herbie shared a prison cell with a black Muslim. In time, the man summed up Herbie in a phrase: "You're not like a lot of other Christians." Herbie took it as a compliment—though it is another sad commentary on how the world perceives us.

There are few people, at least in the Western world, who have not *heard* the Gospel message. So we have to conclude that countless millions either reject it, do not apply it to themselves, or do not regard it as relevant. There are also millions who will never cross the threshold of our churches; as many churches flee the inner cities and head for the high ground of the suburbs, they leave behind people who simply do not feel comfortable enough—or good enough—to come into our handsome sanctuaries.

How then do we break through this cultural barrier and overcome the skepticism and distrust levied toward the evangelicals? Surely that is a priority for us.

The answer lies in obedience. The gritty and sacrificial type that we sometimes, amid our comfortable and cloistered lifestyles, never even consider. But when we Christians take the biblical message to heart and have the courage to *live in obedience to Christ's radical commands*, we are compelled not only to preach the Gospel, but also to take it into the world and live it out. As Saint Francis of Assisi said, "Preach the Gospel all the time; if necessary use words."

Let me give you one example. Jefferson City is a sleepy town of 30,000 people, the capital of Missouri. It is also the site of four state penitentiaries. Most of the inmates come from Kansas City and St. Louis, several hundred miles away.

Every weekend the wives, children, and

families of inmates descend on Jefferson City to visit their loved ones in prison. Most can't afford a motel. Many have been forced to sleep in cars or parking lots or on park benches. There have been some very unfortunate incidents over the years because of the situation.

But in time, Prison Fellowship volunteers saw the needs of these unwanted visitors. They began to invite inmates' families into their homes. That became difficult to manage, however, so a small committee was formed, and an old boarding house located. Volunteers from twelve local churches raised $46,000, bought the home, and with volunteer manpower and contributions, restored it. The sparkling, renovated home officially opened in 1981. Its name? Agape House. And since November 1981 tens of thousands of guests have passed through its doors.

Any night of the week, you will find Agape House full of the wives, children, fathers, and mothers of inmates, who, for a minimal fee, get a clean bed, a Bible, and best of all, a daycare center so children can be cared for while their parents have uninterrupted time together. And one of the most exciting things about Agape House is that it is run by a former

Catholic nun and a Southern Baptist missionary.

In my book *Loving God,* I tell the story of their powerful ministry through the example of a woman I'll call Sherry.

Sherry, who knew the underside of life, worked in a bar, clinging to the thin hope that her husband, sentenced for life, would be released. One evening she was sitting at Agape House's dining room table listening to other prison widows, when the two women of God who manage Agape House came through the room, dispensing towels, asking about husbands, stopping to admire a small child's toy.

Sherry turned away from the conversation and mused, "I don't even know if there is a God. But if He is real and He is good, He must be something like these ladies at Agape House."

You see, my friends, that is not waiting for people to come into our churches or listen to our sermons on radio and television. That is taking the Gospel to them where they are, sharing in their suffering at their point of need, letting them *see* the Good News lived out through God's people.

And when we do this, the world pays attention. Not only does a hardened prisoner's wife like Sherry come to realize that there is a God, but even the secular world can see the difference we Christians make living out our faith. Agape House was even singled out by President Reagan for national recognition in 1982 — as an example to the world of what needs to be done in our communities.

The secular world sees the same thing every time our ministry conducts a community service project — when we take inmates out of prison for two weeks to help the needy, like the project that renovated the home of an elderly Atlanta widow; or the San Antonio project with Habitat for Humanity that built a house for a Spanish-speaking couple with six foster children; or the inmates in Columbia, South Carolina, who refurbished an inner-city playground just before Christmas.

Prison Fellowship is doing these projects all over the country, and each time we do, the secular media sits up and takes notice. They might not cover our church services, but they'll turn out when we invade their territory and make a difference in peoples' lives where they live. The Good News needs to be *seen* as well as heard.

A Future of Promise

What then is our challenge in the decades ahead?

How do we fulfill our biblical commission in an age of unbelief—when orthodoxy is unconsciousness?

1. By being witnesses with the totality of our lives;

2. By discipling others, one-on-one; not just making converts, but training them to live disciplined, holy lives;

3. By breaking out of our comfortable cocoons and engaging the secular world in battle for the hearts and minds of our culture;

4. By strengthening the role of the church, making it truly a holy community;

5. By taking the Gospel into a hostile, skeptical world, living it out for all to see.

An awesome challenge? Yes, indeed. But if God is for us, who can be against us? We, who know a God who is sovereign and at work in history, have no cause for timidity, but have the spirit of "power, love, and a sound mind," as the Apostle Paul wrote to Timothy (2 Timothy 1:7, KJV). We are called to be obedient to One whose will cannot be thwarted.

C.C. Goen, the eminent church historian, wrote of the Reformed tradition, "It bred a race of heroes willing to topple tyrants, carve new kingdoms out of howling wilderness, and erect holy commonwealths to fulfill the righteousness of God on Earth."

Let us be about our business, my brothers and sisters, that we might be found worthy of this, our heritage—and our sovereign Lord's mission for us.

In *Real Christianity*, written late in the eighteenth century and republished in modern English by Multnomah Press, the great Christian parliamentarian and abolitionist leader, William Wilberforce, looked at the world around him. It was a grim picture: Europe awash in tidal waves of humanism caused by the French Revolution, and in England, as Wilberforce wrote, "Infidelity has lifted up her head without shame." But he concluded:

> I must confess equally boldly that my own solid hopes for the well-being of my country depend, not so much on her navies and armies, nor on the wisdom of her rulers, nor on the spirit of her people, as on the persuasion that she still contains many who love

and obey the Gospel of Christ. I believe that their prayers may yet prevail.

There soon followed one of the great revivals of modern time. So too is it my belief that the prayers and work of those who love and obey Christ in our world may yet prevail in a revival the likes of which we've never seen.